Praise for Butterfly:
Chinta

"Thanks for sharing your experiences and your thoughts through this book, Aruna. I am truly inspired and am enthusiastic to live my life with energy and positivity. This book has flown positive energy in me and I am sure it will do the same to everyone who reads it. I am sure every immigrant and non-immigrant will be able to relate to your experiences and thereby connect with you making this world a better place with love and peace."

Subba Marellapudi ~ MBA , PMP
Management Consultant , SAP Risk Systems Functional Lead at KPMG LLP

"This book takes you through a roller coaster of emotions as you laugh and cry along with Aruna's experiences which she narrates with utmost honesty and uncanny precision. The title truly fits, as the book shows the journey of a shy caterpillar coming from its cocoon to a beautiful butterfly, free of worries and bringing joy and peace to everyone it comes in contact with. The insights shared as she went through her spiritual transformation will inspire a common person to not get depressed by the difficult situations faced in life; but to overcome them and mold them as stepping stones for success. Her journey as a single mom gives confidence and inspiration to many others going through similar situations. This book is a very honest and inspiring read and easy to connect with!"

Sreedevi Joshi ~ Principal Engineer, LSI Corp, Allentown PA.

"In this virgin attempt, the author reflects on her life, in all its dimensions and discovers the true meaning and purpose

of relationships that all human beings go through. She vividly describes the role each one of her dear ones played in her life and concludes that if we endeavor to become master of our minds and captain of our hearts we can overcome any sort of hurdles and achieve anything in our lives in any sphere of human activity. I wish her success."

Sudheer Kumar Dundigalla ~ Director, Care College of Pharmacy, Andhra Pradesh, India

"My first word when I read this book was 'WOW, Aruna.' The content has a great balance of emotions and reality. It is very thought provoking and makes you understand the essence of love in anyone's life. This book includes many ideas to convert the negative energy in any human-being into a positive one. I really like the reflections and principles laid out at the end of each chapter. This book has something for everyone, either to learn or to practice. It is full of great food!! Food for your mind and for your body (recipes included)."

Narayana Reddy Thouda ~ Senior Manager ~ SAP Technology, Energy Future Holdings, Dallas TX

"When Aruna came to the Arkansas Teacher Retirement System in 2005, no one could have suspected that she had fought against a life-threatening illness and won. Aruna was so poised and graceful; it would be hard to imagine that she had lead anything but the most pampered life as a daughter and wife. We were wrong in that assumption.

She faced her personal problems with strength and wisdom far beyond her years. What courage it took for her to face the uncertainty of her challenges in a country so far from her home and family. Although young in years, she has the wisdom of someone thrice her age. Each day she faces challenges that few of us will ever know. As chronicled in this book, Aruna demonstrates what the soul of a person can bear and still rise above. It is indeed a privilege to know her. I feel very humble in her presence, and strive to be one-tenth of the person she is."

Gail Bolden ~ Deputy Director, Arkansas Teacher Retirement System

"After reading Butterfly: Journey from My Cocoon I am touched by your life's happenings especially health issues, dealing with married life and raising child as a single mom and your views on life/developing positive attitude. I appreciate the courage and frankness in expressing your life. This book may even help others that are in similar situation and give them strength and show ways to develop positive thinking for moving on with life. Good luck to you and your little one. God Bless!"

Kuchelarao Akkina ~ Director, Customer Service. Customer Service Manager and Project Portfolio Manager at SAIC

"I have had many opportunities to work with and observe Aruna's life and interaction with others. Aruna is a comforting person who is selfless and focused on helping those around her. When she is hurting, she bears that burden with grace. Aruna is constantly building others up and never tearing anyone down. She always has great faith and spirituality as she faces a life problem. She has proven to me that a gentle person can be strong at the same time and do so with dignity and grace. My life will always be better for having worked with Aruna. She is a fine lady in all the right ways."

George Hopkins ~ Director of Arkansas Teacher Retirement System

"Indian history is replete with individuals succeeding against all odds. I am fortunate to know such a person up close, Aruna Chinta. I have witnessed her transform from a shy girl to an amazing public speaker, poised with confidence to take on any challenge she encounters. Aided by her strong will and determination, she not only accepted the challenges life threw at her, but emerged stronger than before. This book not only offers a glimpse at her own journey, but suggests a blueprint for others to keep hopeful during challenging times."

Dora Potluri ~ Technical Consultant

Butterfly

Dear Dan, Beth.

May You and Your Loved ones always be filled with Love, Light, Joy, and Peace!

With Gratitude.

Aruna.

August 8th, 2013.

Butterfly:

Journey from My Cocoon

Aruna Chinta

Butterfly: Journey from My Cocoon
Aruna Chinta

Copyright ©2013 Aruna Chinta

Published by
  Tough Times Never Last Publishing
  Little Rock, Arkansas

All rights reserved. No part of this book may be reproduced in whole or in part without written permission from the publisher, except by a reviewer who may quote brief passages in a review; nor may any part of the book be reproduced, stored in a retrieval system or transmitted in any form or by any means, electronic or mechanical, including photocopying, recording or other, without prior written permission of the publisher.

This publication is designed to provide accurate and authoritative information in regard to the subject matter covered. It is sold with the understanding that the publisher is not engaged in rendering professional medical services. If professional advice or other expert assistance is required, the services of a competent professional should be sought. The name of Aruna's former husband has been changed to protect his identity.

The pure intent of this book is to inspire and give hope that life can be lived in joy, grace and peace. The author or the publishing company holds no responsibility nor is liable to any person or entity with respect to any information shared in this book.

ISBN: 978-0-9791071-0-8
ISBN: 0-9791071-0-5

Cover design by Gerry Castro and Crystal McMahon
Page design by Quality Data Mill, Pvt Ltd
Aruna's photo by Portrait Innovations
Production coordination by Jan M. Whalen, MASL

Printed in the United States of America

This book is dedicated to my family—
Ammamma, Amma, Daddy, Jyothi Pinni,
Anna, Vadina, Akka, Bavagaru, Gautam, Mamata,
nieces Mona and Sindhu, nephews Abhi and Pranav
and my son, Keshav—
for giving me roots to grow and wings to fly,
being with me through my thick and thin times,
multiplying my joy and laughter, dividing my pain and sorrow
and for who they are.
They mean everything to me.
I offer my deepest gratitude and love.

Table of Contents

Preface	xiii
Introduction	xvii
Part 1: My Brush with Death	1
Part 2: My Marriage	35
Part 3: Spiritual Transformation	65
Part 4: Raising My Son	103
Final Thoughts	135
Glossary of Telugu Terms	141
Acknowledgements	145
About the Author	151

Preface

I was born and raised in India. Our family was traditional, with family values and culture deeply embedded in its core. I was given the freedom to choose my own path. I was a typical timid girl—sweet and responsible, yet dependent and always seeking acceptance from others. Being the youngest of three siblings, I was the most pampered and always won the most attention, affection and guidance from my siblings and parents. I was also the target of many jokes. My naivety and slow nature often evoked some good laughs and fun in our family. It didn't take very long for me to earn the nickname "tubelight," as it used to take ages for a joke to sink in. The nickname still holds true to date, but perhaps I've just become a much *brighter* tubelight, rather than a *faster* tubelight.

Of the three siblings, Akka, my sister who is five years older than me, is the eldest in the family, and Anna, my brother, the middle child, is two years older. I was raised by my maternal grandparents between the ages of 1 and 3. My mother is the second oldest child in her family and most of her seven siblings were unmarried and living with my grandparents at that time. So, I was raised affectionately not just by my grandparents but also by my pinnilu (mom's sisters) and mamalu (mom's brothers).

I still have good childhood memories of all our summer vacations and some major festivals celebrated in Ammamma's (my mother's mom) village. My Ammamma is a loving, beautiful person—still very young at heart and

BUTTERFLY

very dear to kith and kin of all ages. Her progeny extends to seven children, eighteen grandchildren and sixteen great grandchildren (to date).

I am blessed with wonderful parents. I don't remember being brought up with any rules dictated by my parents. Rather, they taught us many things just from the way they lived. What else could be a better teaching tool than being a great role model? Dad is a well-disciplined person who always sticks to his values. If Dad gives his word, people can rely on it more than on any promissory note. Dad is a diligent worker and pays work as much reverence as he pays God.

Dad is a strong-willed, yet soft and unassuming man. He has great determination and will-power to rise up to do whatever is needed even in the most challenging and trying times. At the same time, he is kind, gentle and compassionate to his fellow man and offers his tender, loving care in the most humble way. Having lost his father when he was only ten, Dad had to shoulder the responsibility of providing for his mother, youngest brother and youngest sister. He faced many challenges—as young boy. In spite of it all, he fulfilled his responsibilities gracefully.

Dad took a break in studies, worked as a full-time employee to meet the family's financial needs and later pursued a bachelor of engineering degree, which was one of the most prestigious and hard-earned degrees in those days. He always encouraged us in our studies, and to this day he keeps supporting the education of children and college students by contributing a part of his retirement income to financially under-privileged children. He is also engaged with the students' progress at school and with their families. He remains in touch with them as they go along with their life's journey.

Amma (mom) is a loving mother, tender-hearted, gentle and very soft-spoken, who devotes her life to nurturing children and now grandchildren as well. She would take care

Preface

of all the activities at home. While Dad was the sole breadwinner of the family, Amma's job as a housewife was not inferior, and I feel it is a much bigger job than what I have working outside the home. We always had Amma's freshly-cooked meals and homemade snacks; one of the biggest contributing factors to our good health.

My siblings were also my friends with whom I played during my childhood; I didn't have friends of my own. Their friends were my friends and playmates too. The streets in front of our houses used to be the playgrounds. We didn't have sibling rivalry, partly because a boy was spaced between the two girls. Both my Anna and Akka used to protect and take care of me in different ways. I had fun teasing and playing with Anna and received elderly guidance and girl-talks from Akka.

My first time away from home, family and siblings was when I joined the Jawaharlal Nehru Technological University, Anantapur, in my home state of Andhra Pradesh for my bachelor's in engineering. Journeys to home used to be a nine-hour bus trips, so I went home only once every month or so. It gave me the first experiences of being outside my loving home. I learned to take care of certain things by myself, yet in a supportive environment provided by friends. Spending four years together, having common academic goals, being independent from parents and on our own gave us ample opportunities to build good friendships—probably the best friendships of my life. Fortunately, I am still in touch with these friends even after parting from college 17 years ago, of course, thanks to Facebook! I wasn't ever the gregarious, extroverted type, but rather a shy, timid person in my own cocoon when around those I didn't know, but with the few close friends, I was a chatterbox confiding everything.

Growing up, I really didn't have to go through any struggles or challenges, as most things were taken care of for me by my family. I just went with the flow of life. I was content, happy and comfortable in my own cocoon. Using Anna as a role model in education, I decided on my own to follow his path of studying engineering, so I received my bachelor's degree, then came to the United States to pursue a master's and to work in information technology. Of course, I'm not the intelligent student he is, nor did I struggle through the financial or emotional challenges as he had during his pursuit of his master's degree in a different country. He was there to support and guide me when I came to US.

I came to the United States in December of 1996 to study for my master's. I had just taken the TOEFL and GRE, with the help of my brother who had gone through this process. He also helped me with the application process. I happily stepped into graduate school at the University of Texas, Arlington. After one year, I wanted to take up a full-time job rather than focusing on my master's. So I started my career as a software programmer and have continued in the same field.

I got married in February of 1999 and moved from Dallas to New Jersey to join my husband. He was from the same part of southern India as I was and our mother tongue was the same. Though our family came to know about him through both parents, what I find interesting is that the marriage was my choice rather than the decision of the whole family, which is not customary. At times it still surprises me how I made such a big decision, by myself because until then I was always dependent on my loved ones even for petty decisions.

I guess some things in life happen the way they happen for a reason. Now, I can see I am totally responsible for my life, totally responsible for the way I lived and totally responsible for the way I am living now. A few years down the line I would see even more clearly how my current living contributes to making my future life.

Introduction

Facing a life-threatening illness in the year 2000, followed by a five-year break from work, gave me an opportunity to pause and reflect on my life—discovering my life's purpose. All these experiences also deepened my spirituality and belief in the Supreme Powers. This journey of self-discovery liberated me and gave me wings to face the world with confidence and poise.

This book is a humble attempt to share my story. If it gives wings to anyone to fly even a tad higher than where they are now, my purpose is served.

What do *you* consider the key to living a life of joy and freedom? My philosophy is: accepting 100 percent responsibility for one's life. It's totally up to me to make my life the way I want it to be. I didn't always feel this way. Only when I believed and accepted this truth did I start to find the means and ways to become what I wanted to be. I'd like to share my discoveries with you.

I started by counting my myriad of blessings. I have wonderful parents, ideal siblings and an adorable baby boy. I am blessed with a job where people appreciate me and my work. It's like a second home—the place where I spend most of my day. I cherish my co-workers who are also my good friends and help me in several ways. I treasure my local and long-distance friends who are there for me to talk to when I need support. They guide me in decision making and encourage me to continue to reach my goals.

Butterfly

I've never had any limitations to becoming what I wanted to be. However, a transformational shift happened in me only when I encountered a few major events in my life. These events made me an even better, finer and a more confident person.

The transformation, progress and achievements I experienced do not compare to the accomplishments of the great achievers of the world. What I see in myself and my achievements are not on par, and could even be considered a minute speck in comparison with the greatest, noblest, inspiring deeds of many outstanding achievers. Rather, I am comparing my "new" self with my "old" self, from living in a cocoon to becoming a butterfly.

My transformation began with two major events. Both have impacted me, building in me strength, courage and determination in their own ways. But, I can say that I dramatically transformed myself with the second event when I accepted complete responsibility for my life and my baby's life.

These events brought a true transformation in me. What is even more exhilarating is—this transformation is not limited to an event, rather, the transformation happened within *Me*. It changed my core personality, the thinking patterns, the behavioral patterns and the way I perceive and respond to people and events.

I discovered that I was passively letting my life happen *to* me. Now, I am making my life happen *for* me. It's a one-word difference, but that difference has allowed my life to take flight.

With any transformation we undergo, we view the world differently. We can experience joy and bliss in each of the simple things. We can handle situations more effectively, with inner strength, courage, balance and peace. We can find a good lesson out of every encounter. When you fly above the situation, you have a clearer perspective.

INTRODUCTION

Life has left me with some beautiful, insightful lessons. I expect miracles, and certainly they keep flowing my way. Miracles are not reserved for bigger, greater things. They are found and experienced in everyday little things. We just have to take time to recognize and cherish them. We all deserve to live an absolutely gorgeous life, to enjoy each moment in the best possible way—just as free, happy butterflies.

I firmly believe in the words of the late Dr. Norman Vincent Peale: "Problems are pearls of great price. The greater the problem, the greater the value of the pearl ..." If our lives were all smooth and rosy, we would have not experience growth to this extent. I would have stayed safely in my cocoon, my comfort shell. But that is definitely not what you or I were born for. I believe there is a higher purpose set for each person.

Though my journey was not always hurdle free, I am proud of the person I have become in the process ... the lessons I learned and the personal growth I attained. Whatever situations we are in, by rising above, and spreading our wings, we can get onto much higher planes and experience abundance of love, joy, peace and bliss.

Part 1:
My Brush with Death

Part 1
My Brush with Death

The story of my brush with death began on August 21, 2000, just a year and a half after my marriage to Anil.

It was Monday morning when Anil, took me to a family practitioner, Dr. Suseela Botlagudur. We had just returned home to New Jersey on Saturday night after a two-week trip to India. We attended the wedding of Anil's younger brother. My feet were swollen. The swelling started during the 20-hour long flight to India. Though I've never had this kind of problem before on any of my previous flights to and from India, I wasn't alarmed. I thought it was common for feet to swell—Daddy and also Akka (my elder sister) experienced this during their long flights. But mine remained swollen for the whole two weeks we were in India until we returned back home.

Now we were here in the waiting room until the doctor could see me. Luckily, I had the first appointment of the day so it wasn't a long wait.

As the doctor walked in, giving a warm handshake, she looked closely into my face. "Your lips are looking very pale as if your hemoglobin is low."

With a smile, I answered, "Oh, my lips, many times, look that way and it could be misleading."

She asked why I was there, and so I went over my symptoms. I started with my current symptoms of swollen feet, urinary incontinence and a bit of a reeling sensation, especially while climbing down the stairs. Also, I had some not so predominant symptoms, such as tiredness, especially after returning home from work, and a suffocating feeling, especially in the kitchen. I handed over the reports of the tests I'd had in India. She looked through them and ordered new tests.

I didn't know if it was important, but I also told her that I worked 12 to 16 hours a day for about a five-month period. I didn't pay much attention then, but realized how difficult it was after my working hours came down to eight- to ten-hour days.

The week passed by pretty quickly catching up with work, unpacking bags from the India trip and getting back into a routine. When I spoke to Anna (my elder brother), who worked for an airline company, he mentioned that he sent me a buddy pass to fly to Dallas for a short visit. My parents were visiting Anna, and Amma was about to go to Oman to be with my pregnant Akka. Anna said, "Aruna, I thought you would like to see Amma, and we all wanted to see you as well. Can you fly this Friday evening after work?"

Without a second's thought, I said, "Of course!" I was elated.

On Friday evening, Anil dropped me off at Newark Airport. It had been about three months since I'd seen my parents and a year since I'd seen my Anna and Vadina (my sister-in-law). My Vadina was pregnant with her first child and I was excited to see her.

My trip was just a short visit—from Friday to Sunday—but when it comes to family, the little time we get to spend together is still warm and special. We finally found time to sit and chat after dinner that night. Time flew by talking about my India trip. I casually mentioned that I had been feeling occasional fatigue and weakness—especially in my legs. Everyone got a bit concerned. "It could be due to hectic

My Brush with Death

schedule, the India trip and not getting enough rest," said Anna, trying to lower our anxiety. I mentioned that I had seen a doctor early this week and had yet to hear the results. Anna said, "Please keep us posted, Aruna."

Sunday morning, Anna went to Kroger's grocery store to get a whole chicken and some yummy Indian sweets and snacks. He cooked the chicken himself, packed it for me and said, "You don't need to cook after going home. Eat and go to bed early tonight."

I made it back home Sunday evening with no problems.

Monday morning while I was at work I received a call from my doctor saying that my hemoglobin count was 7.3 and that she wanted to repeat the test. Normally, my hemoglobin used to be about 12. I went back to the clinic for another test on Tuesday morning and was called back in a few hours saying my hemoglobin was still 7.3 and I needed to be seen by a hematologist. In the mean time she prescribed rest and to take off from work.

The Hematologist appointment was set for August 31 at 1:15 p.m. I remember that day quite well. Anil was scheduled to arrive by train to the nearby Piscataway station at 12:30 p.m. It was his last day of work in New York City. He turned in his resignation right after we returned from India. His intent in leaving the job was to change to a different field by learning new skills.

I made cabbage stir fry and tomato pappu (dal). I packed his lunch and took it to the station and afterward we went to my hematologist appointment together.

This Hematologist's name is Janaki Giri, a middle-aged Indian woman. She performed a CBC and ran the test herself in the lab. My hemoglobin count was even lower—7.1. She ordered a bone marrow biopsy.

"Bone marrow biopsy?" My thoughts went to my paternal uncle who went through a life-threatening illness, with several bone marrow procedures. I recalled that it is a painful procedure.

"Can we wait for a while? Maybe if I get some good rest and eat iron-rich foods, it will help to improve my blood counts."

With a weak smile, she said, "No, this is not something that could be improved with rest or diet. To know the reason for these low blood counts, I need to do a bone marrow biopsy, where I will be taking marrow from your bone with a needle. Similar to how blood is drawn from veins, marrow is drawn from your bone marrow. You will be given a local anesthesia. It is a simple procedure and is done in less than 15 minutes. You will have pain for a day or two and will need some help to cope."

She looked at the schedule and offered the date of September 6 as the earliest available, as there was a holiday for Labor Day weekend the following week. It was scheduled at the JFK Medical Center in New Jersey.

On our way back home, I called Anna and mentioned this. I could sense that he was a bit alarmed. Anna asked if we could fax my test results to him, so Anil sent them from a local copy store on our way home.

ENERGY TRAVELS! ANNA HEARD ME!

After reaching home, Anil said he had a headache and needed to sleep for some time. I sat in the living room by myself. I was a bit sad. I remembered that Amma would be leaving tomorrow to be with Akka in Oman. My eyes got wet missing Amma. I wasn't really worried or thinking of anything, but tears rolled off my cheeks uncontrollably. Just then my phone rang. It was Anna.

He asked me how I was doing, and I told him I was doing well. Then he announced, "Amma is coming to your place tomorrow afternoon."

My Brush with Death

"What?" I was startled and filled with mixed emotions. "Amma is leaving for Akka's place tomorrow, right?"

"No, Aruna, she is not. I am postponing her ticket and making arrangements for Amma to fly to your place tomorrow."

Suddenly, all that gloominess disappeared and I was filled with thoughts of Amma coming to see me. I felt a warm comfort.

The next afternoon we went to the Newark Airport to pick up Amma. It seemed like a long wait. Finally, Amma walked out of the plane and seeing her I tried to get up with little support and slight difficulty. Seeing me struggle, she had a worried look. So I tried to cheer her up with a big smile on my face. We walked out of the terminal chatting and Anil went to the parking lot to bring the car to the curb side.

The weather was indeed nice for this first day of September. Winter hadn't commenced yet, and it was not hot either. It was just the perfect temperature to be out, so we wanted to relish this weather. We rolled our windows down on the local roads and enjoyed the fresh breeze.

Amma stayed with me for two weeks. I thoroughly enjoyed my time with her as if I were a child again. Now I was home all day as my doctor said not to go to work. Amma and I would spend the day chatting and relaxing with no pressures of waking up early or finishing the chores at home. Amma was doing everything for me and I was happy to have this opportunity and time to spend with her.

It's surprising how emotions play a role in our lives. When we are feeling down, they can either empower us or crush us. It looked like I am gaining physical strength now with Amma's arrival. Amma and I went for short, slow walks and I enjoyed the nice warm, yummy food she prepared for me. One day we even went shopping and then to the laundromat to wash several loads of clothes, including all comforters and we had a good time folding them together. These are undeniably small things, yet they comforted me in that time of my unknown future.

First Bone Marrow Biopsy: September 6, 2000

Amma accompanied me to my first bone marrow procedure. I was glad that Anil drove us to the JFK Medical Center. Being the first appointment of the day, the doctor was on time and I was out in less than 15 minutes. It wasn't bad at all. Not as painful as I imagined. I felt the pressure of the procedure more than pain. I came out walking by myself with a smile. Looking at the very concerned, nervous look on my Amma's face I smiled even more and said, "I am doing great, Amma. It isn't really hurting."

Within a few minutes, Anna called to check on me. I spoke with great cheer and told him that I was not in pain. I had a happy and relieved feeling that the procedure was over. We came home. We had a long walkway from the parking lot to our apartment. As I started lifting myself out of the car, I felt some pain. Still it wasn't too bad.

With Amma's help, I made it to the bathroom and then made it to the couch. Now the pain was increasing. It then struck me—I didn't feel any pain so far because of the anesthesia. Aha! Now I was ready for the painkillers that the doctor prescribed. After lunch, I felt a bit drowsy, so I slept for a few hours. When I woke up, I felt an excruciating pain. I found it so hard to move, tears came rolling down my cheeks.

The doctor had said that the biopsy specimen would be sent to the pathology laboratory and we'd be receiving the results by end of the week or early next week. But it took much longer than we expected. The doctor wanted me to come into her clinic the following Friday to repeat my blood work.

My Brush with Death

The results were shocking. My hemoglobin lowered even more—to 6.7. She prescribed some iron capsules. They drew several syringes of blood. Looking at it, Amma anxiously asked, "You are already anemic and how come they are drawing so much blood?"

I smiled at Amma's innocent question and said, "Amma, normally it takes just few hours for the body to reproduce this amount of blood." But secretly I was a little worried. We were still waiting on my pathology results of the bone marrow biopsy. Why was it taking so long?

Amma's plan to go to Akka's place was not part of my parents' original plan. They came to the States to visit Anna and Vadina, to offer emotional support and to help with the newborn. Vadina was due to have the baby in the second week of October. My parents' visitor visa was valid for a maximum of six months and they were required to return to India by November.

Akka and her family had moved to Sultanate of Oman, a country they weren't at all familiar with. They chose to move as my Bavagaru, who's a Doctor, got a really good opportunity to work there. Akka was pregnant with her second child and coincidentally, shared the same due date as Vadina. As Akka started having complications, Amma decided to go to Oman to be of support and help to Akka.

Anna postponed Amma's scheduled flight from September 1 to September 23 to have her by my side during bone marrow procedure. I guess he was able to gauge the enormity of the procedure. We were hoping to have the biopsy results by the time Amma had to leave and hoped it wouldn't be anything complicated. Almost two weeks passed and no results yet. Why was it taking so long?

On the 21, the doctor asked me to come in for an appointment. She repeated my blood work and my hemoglobin had dropped again—to 6.4. She said that I needed a blood transfusion and scheduled it for the following week. Still no word about my pathology reports. At one point, I overheard Anil's conversation with the doctor, but I couldn't really make out any words. My anxiety rose.

The doctor came back and said, "Get good rest and take good care of yourself. You will be feeling more energetic after your blood transfusion." I asked her when I could go back to work. With a feeble smile she said, "Don't worry about it. With the letter I gave you earlier, you won't be working until I give the approval."

I asked Anil what the doctor told him. He didn't say anything. A few minutes later, I asked him one more time. He said, "Nothing. She just asked you to rest." Still, it kept nagging me and I asked one last time after coming home. I got the same reply—with more coldness. Why didn't he talk to me? But I wasn't feeling strong enough to take it further so I dropped it from my mind.

By then, Amma had flown back to Dallas in preparation for her overseas trip. She gave me comforting news when she called "Daddy will be coming tomorrow. Stay well until then. He will take care of all your needs. I will be back soon after Akka delivers the baby." We ended the phone call in good cheerful tones, making each other feel better.

The next day, I noticed my energy was decreasing. Simple tasks like walking around the house to take care of myself or going to the bathroom were not easy anymore. I experienced pain in my knees. I did better in the morning but as the day progressed, I noticed my steps getting crooked and my walk was getting clumsier. I was so exhausted. I literally did nothing but lay on the couch, reading a bit of my technical books. I slept a lot. I didn't feel anything really painful or alarming but why was I not feeling my usual energetic self? Why was I getting exhausted so quickly?

My Brush with Death

Daddy arrived and after a brief chat, quickly plunged into the dinner preparations for me. I laughed, "What, *you* will cook?"

With a big smile and a confident tone, Daddy said, "Why not? I used to cook some for myself when you were little and Amma used to go to your Ammamma's (my mother's mother) place for long vacations."

"Oh, that was more than 24 years back!" I started laughing. He finished preparing dinner and surprised me with his cooking. He made some yummy pappu and rasam. We had a hearty chat and a warm dinner.

After dinner, Daddy looked at both Anil and me and told us that Anna would be calling us the next day at 2 p.m. He said, "Let's finish our lunch early before then and keep this time open." I nodded, but why did he need an appointment to talk to us?

The next day, Daddy reminded us of the phone call and all three of us finished our lunch early. Daddy and I relaxed on the couch. I was in great spirits, eagerly waiting for Anna's call, but Anil got up and walked out of the room, as if he were looking for something. He seemed unsettled but didn't say anything. He didn't return until later that afternoon.

Revealing the Diagnosis

To prepare me, Daddy carefully started giving me information about the purpose of Anna's call. "Anna spoke to your doctor over the phone. She said that the bone marrow biopsy report showed a one percent chance of the presence of hairy cell leukemia."

"Leukemia?" I was startled. "That means blood cancer, right?"

He started assuring me, "Yes, but now technology has grown so much and we have a cure for many diseases.

It should be a pretty simple one and you will be going into remission pretty quickly."

I wasn't sad or upset. Since I am a person with slow reactions, like a tubelight, some things don't sink in very soon. In this case it happened to be an advantage.

Anna called sharply at 2 p.m. He said he spoke to Dr. Giri and was told about the diagnosis. Then he said the treatment included chemotherapy.

He said, "More than the procedure, you need to be very strong emotionally. This treatment might kill some of the healthy cells in addition to the harmful cells. Because of this, there might be some psychological and physiological disturbances. So it is really important that you have good emotional support to handle it well. It would be good if you move to Dallas. This would make it easier for all of us, including our parents to better support each other."

He continued, "I've researched this and UT Southwestern Hospital in Dallas is supposed to offer the best treatment; they focus on the latest research. I approached the chief of the bone marrow transplants, Dr. Robert Collins, and discussed your case with him. He graciously accepted to see you and made on appointment for you for October 6."

He continued further, "Once you have your blood transfusion, you will get some energy to handle the trip to Dallas. Until then, try to rest and take good care of yourself. Let Daddy take care of you and help you with all activities. Daddy and you can fly as soon as your transfusion is over."

After Anna's call, slowly things started sinking in. Lot of thoughts started coming in at once. It was too much information and I was trying to think straight. Then I said, "Daddy, keep my things separate. Don't mix up my cup, plate, spoon and fork."

Daddy smiled, "It's not contagious, Aruna."

I started voicing my thoughts, "Daddy, I am not comfortable being with Anna's family at this time. They will be

My Brush with Death

having a little one soon, something to be happy and joyous about. I don't want to be around them when I am sick. It will be an added burden for Anna and Vadina."

He reassured me, "I will make sure that there is no extra burden to Anna and Vadina. I will handle all your needs. When Amma comes back, it will be even easier. By being close to Anna's family, we will have good emotional support and any help we need to drive us to the doctor or the hospital."

Anna called again later to convince me, "Aruna, we would be feeling more at peace with you next to us so that we can see you personally. It worries us more when you are staying at a distance." So I agreed to come to Dallas.

Daddy then revealed how Amma was unwilling to go to Oman after hearing my diagnosis. It seems she was completely in tears and didn't want to go away leaving me in this state.

Then Dad assured Amma, "I will take care of Aruna not just as a father but as a mother as well. I will do whatever you would have done for her. Anyway it will take some time to evaluate Aruna's results before the treatment can be started. By that time, you will be back here when she needs you the most." Reluctantly, Mom had agreed to go to Oman.

First Blood Transfusion

Soon, the day of the transfusion came. We made it to the hospital well before appointment time. At first there was some nervousness until the process started. It began by poking me with needles to find a good vein. Daddy was sitting by me with a brave face. Nurses and doctors kept monitoring me more frequently as this was my first transfusion.

We rented a nice Indian movie, "Annamaya", to watch during my transfusion. It was a good movie to pass time pleasantly. I noticed Anil filling out some paperwork. When

BUTTERFLY

I checked with him later he said that he was filling out a lease document to rent an apartment in Dallas. This was in the same complex as Anna's family. I was happy and to hear that he made the decision so quickly, and a decision which was comforting to me at that time.

The transfusion went on for about seven hours. We were glad it went well and there was a big sigh of relief after the long process was over. We reached home and went to bed early that night as it was exhausting with all the extra attention we had to have in the process.

Anna had booked flights for Daddy and me for the next afternoon. He told us that an apartment was available in the same complex and we could move in the following week. Anil planned to move after packing and shipping all our belongings.

Daddy packed all my clothes and my personal belongings. He didn't pack them in his usual way, rather, he packed them in the exact way I do, according to my taste and instructions. You can imagine how it is to adhere to someone else's way of doing things, especially if that someone is very picky and detail oriented.

I was not sure if I could really make the next day's flight. I couldn't even gather the energy to move around at home. How would I do in the flight? How would I walk to the terminal in the airport? How would I get up the stairs at Anna's place? Daddy also seemed to be physically exhausted.

The next morning I got up, ate my breakfast and fell back to sleep. I was feeling better, but still fatigued. Daddy arranged for everything and woke me up. He helped me get ready, combed my hair and fed me. Suddenly, as if a higher energy pervaded through me, I said, "Okay, Daddy, let's make this trip. We will go. I am feeling good."

Actually, I had no trouble at the airport or during the flight. I didn't even need a wheelchair after getting off the

My Brush with Death

plane. Anna came to the airport to pick us up. And I walked up the stairs to his apartment just fine.

A few things make me wonder now. How did my energy transform so quickly? Did I act like I was weak? Is it really an emotional state or do I receive unknown positive energies just when I need them? I don't have an answer to any of these questions, so it is still amazing.

There was a big sigh of relief when I arrived at Anna's home. Anna and Vadina felt much better to see me face to face rather than imagining how I was, just talking over the phone from a long distance. Dad felt relieved too, as he had Anna by his side now. We all slept with much comfort and peace.

Within two days, on October 6, I had my appointment with Dr. Collins at UT Southwestern Medical Center. Anna, Daddy and I went together. The doctor came in to examine me. He was a tall, slim gentleman with a warm handshake. He went over my details, symptoms and history.

The doctor excused himself and requested a few minutes to study my case. He came back and said that he would like to do a bone marrow biopsy because he felt that the previous one did not give conclusive results. He asked if it was okay to go for it now and I nodded yes. Within a few minutes, everything was set up for the procedure.

The doctor and his nurse were in the room with me; Anna and Daddy were waiting outside. I was given a local anesthesia to numb that area, the top ridge of my right hipbone in the back. It was going slow and I felt the pressure. I remember each step of that day as if it were yesterday. The doctor checked in every few minutes—I felt some pain. I sensed it was taking longer but had no idea how long. The doctor said he would give me a little more numbing medicine as he needed to go deeper. I felt more and more pain and started getting tense.

When it was finally over, I said, "Thank you, Doctor." He said, sympathetically, "Thank you so much for taking this much pain. I am so sorry I had to hurt you. I couldn't get the marrow on the periphery so I had to go deeper and deeper. I am still not sure if we got enough. But that is the best I could do. I will send the marrow specimen to pathology and we will call you once the results are back."

Looking at the clock, I realized that this procedure took 45minutes. The doctor and nurse helped me sit up and I knew Anna and Daddy would be in soon. With a concerned look, Anna approached me and asked, "How are you doing, Aruna?"

I couldn't hold my emotions any longer and started crying silently with no words. It concerned Anna and Daddy. Within a few minutes I gained my composure and said, "It's hurting. I am fine though."

Once I got home, I found some comfort and relief. Not that the pain subsided; I guess I was getting used to it. Daddy sat by me day and night with extra attentiveness. Anna and Vadina too were checking on me and helping me. By the following evening, I got some relief from the extreme pain and I was able to sit up and chat comfortably. The same night, Vadina went into labor and was taken to the hospital. A baby girl was born!

The arrival of my precious little niece, Sindhu, certainly brought big smiles, joy and vibrant positive spirits to our whole family. Looking at the little one and spending time with her certainly took our minds off the stress and anxiety. On the third day after she was born, we received a call from Amma that Akka delivered her baby too. Both mom and child were doing well!

Anil arrived in Dallas and we moved into the new apartment. Daddy was traveling back and forth between Anna's apartment and my apartment. He brought in food, joined us

MY BRUSH WITH DEATH

for all the hospital visits and stayed with me whenever Anil stepped out.

Looking back, I wonder how that huge step of moving and changing our home, from New Jersey to Dallas, happened so quickly. Now that I think about it, I guess things just started aligning themselves into place, and that big step culminated without much thought. Perhaps two things helped Anil make this decision: he was out of job and the fact that a Dallas based company had initially sponsored his H1B immigration. He could continue to work for this company for another client. So this move happened with absolutely no resistance—relatively without effort.

Similarly, many other blessings came to me. My parents coming to the US at that time, Anna arranging for Amma to be with me during my bone-marrow biopsy, Amma postponing her trip to Akka's place, Dad being with me when Amma had to go Oman, Anna researching doctors and choosing this particular hospital—UTSW and wonderful Dr.Collins, Anna suggesting us to move to Dallas to offer me all possible help and support. These things happened seamlessly!

Each of these steps indeed was crucial. Under normal circumstances, they require lots of planning, thinking and are bound by financial and logistical constraints. But I guess, under extreme situations, extreme decisions happen by just being sensible, compassionate and pulling everything together.

Whenever I think about all this, I am overcome with positive emotions. I believe everything happened effortlessly and gracefully because each of my dear family members was open, receptive and fully connected to the Higher-Consciousness. They were certainly driven by the omniscient and omnipotent Almighty. There's just no way all these events would have aligned so smoothly and impeccably. It is hard to even imagine how and where I would have been now without all these blessings. I strongly believe that in life, when one door closes, there is always another one opening.

Within a week's time we received a call from Dr. Collins that my bone marrow biopsy results came in but they didn't have a conclusive diagnosis. On a positive note, he ruled out hairy cell leukemia. I needed to go for an MRI of my legs as I complained of pain in my knees and shins. He also mentioned that I would be scheduled for a bone scan. He would monitor me with frequent blood work once or twice a week.

The day of my MRI came. Thank God for the open MRIs we have today! I didn't like staying still inside a horizontal tunnel and the frequent loud banging noises were bothering me—it was so claustrophobic. I felt like screaming out loud and breaking out of that enclosed tunnel. The MRI was over in 45 minutes. I thought that the painful sticking of needles is much better than this MRI!

The MRI results came in pretty quickly. The doctor said they found that 80 percent of the bone is scarred in areas just below the kneecap, so he wanted me to undergo an orthopedic surgery. They would cut an incision and take a scoop of marrow from my shin as he couldn't get a substantial marrow specimen during the bone marrow biopsy. He said his nurse would arrange an appointment with an orthopedic surgeon.

I was scheduled for this appointment with Dr. Fennigan on November 13, the day Amma planned to return from Oman.

Amma's Return—My Second Transfusion

I was excited about Amma's coming back and yet concerned as to how she would respond when she sees me. My energy levels were so much higher the last time she saw me.

My Brush with Death

This was when I went to the airport to give her a sendoff. Now I was no longer that way. It is not that I was bedridden—I still had good energy levels but they kept fluctuating. I used to feel good after a night's sleep and post my naps. I would have relatively more energy in the morning and it would wane as the day progressed.

My walks were a clear indication of my energy level. My steps would get awkward and clumsy. Again, it may not have been noticeably obvious to someone else but I'd feel it. I'd notice my hands losing strength. I'd do most things normally but that wouldn't be for very long. Even holding my dinner plate for too long became a burden; it seemed like the weight of the plate was pulling it down and making me drop it. The threshold levels were diminishing. There wasn't much of a time lapse from when I realized I was getting weak until it became unbearable.

Fortunately, all my family members were sensitive to notice this and started taking care of me accordingly. Even holding my precious niece, as much as I loved to do it, wasn't possible for more than a few minutes. Anna and Vadina would give her to me to play with and cuddle. They would keep watching me and take her back just before the pain became too much. Many times I wondered how they attuned themselves to know me and my expressions without my telling them explicitly. Were they my mind readers or was my pain showing through so obviously?

My energy levels had risen after my transfusion in NY. Now, after four weeks, they were again progressively diminishing. I was afraid I would seem lethargic by the time Amma comes. *It would be nice if I could get another transfusion just before Amma's arrival.* As if someone had just heard my thoughts, my doctor's nurse, Katie, called to tell me that my blood transfusion appointment was set for November 10.

Butterfly

Amma's Arrival and Orthopedic Appointment, November 13, 2000

I was elated. Amma's flight arrived at noon. I had my appointment with the orthopedic surgeon that afternoon. We picked her up, ate our lunch and got to my appointment. Dr. Fennigan, the orthopedic surgeon, went over what she would be doing and the details of the procedure.

Making a circle with the tips of her index and thumb touching, she said, "I will cut a hole about this big and take a scoop of marrow. Our intent is to get a good amount of marrow specimen to help with the evaluation and diagnosis." She also showed me where she would be operating. It was on my right leg, just below my knee cap. Always thinking ahead, Anna asked, "Are there any special things we need to know before the procedure and care after surgery?"

"You will be given an instruction sheet of the diet she needs before the surgery. After the surgery, she will be in quite a bit of pain. She will be given some pain medication to use for a few days."

Dad anxiously asked, "How can she walk up the stairs to the second floor after the surgery?"

"Hmm, good question. The best way I can think of is, make her sit on the bottom stair and help her to scoot up one step at a time."

Ortho Surgery, November 20, 2000

A few days before the orthopedic surgery Anna requested, "Aruna, it will be nice if you stay with us after the surgery. You will need more help, and it will be easy for all of us to be involved and help if you stay with us." I agreed, as I knew Anil couldn't give me all the support I needed all by himself.

My family was with me—Amma, Daddy, Anna and Anil. I was put on a stretcher, given anesthesia and taken

My Brush with Death

into the operating room. The last thing I remember before my sedated eyes completely shut was the glimmering view of the operating room. It seemed like a huge mechanical workshop with robust machines spread all over. Certainly, it didn't seem like the sophisticated operating room I'd seen on the television show "ER". I could be wrong, but that's the glimpse I had from my semi-conscious state, before my eyelids completely closed and I dropped off into nowhere. By the time I came back to a conscious state, I was in the middle of the hallway surrounded by my family.

I was drenched in pain. The nurses came in saying they needed to move me. They put me in a wheelchair and began to help me to bend my legs and keep them on the chair rest. I felt inside, don't they understand what I was going through? I was in terrible pain—I couldn't move even a hundredth of an inch. I begin to cry. Amma and Anna comfort me, and I felt a lot better emotionally.

In the midst of that painful time, a memory flashed through my mind and I looked at Anna and said, "It's my turn."

He gave me a puzzled expression. "Your turn? What are you saying?"

I smiled at the thought of our life as children in India. When I was six years old, Akka hit an electric pole while playing and was injured near her eye. Daddy and Amma rushed Akka to the hospital and she returned home a few hours later with four stitches. It took two weeks to heal, but we were glad her eye wasn't permanently injured.

A couple of months passed, and one day, Anna, this dear brother who stands by me right now, didn't show up during our lunch break at school. I asked Kollapudi, the guy who brings us lunch, where he was. He told me that Anna didn't come to school today because on his way to school, he had an accident. A motor bike hit the cycle Anna was sitting

BUTTERFLY

on. Fortunately, it was nothing major. I couldn't wait to go home to see the stitches on his lip.

I turned to Anna and said, "Since the day of your accident, a thought had been running through my head. Akka got stitches. Anna got stitches. So, it's my turn next, but when is this going to be? Secretly, this thought made my heart anxious and I carried it through my life. Surely this operation counts as *my turn*."

He smiled. I burst into laughter remembering the silly panicked thoughts I was holding since my childhood. A peaceful relief came as we prepared to go back home.

The next ordeal was climbing up the stairs to the second floor. It was winter time and pretty cold outside. Daddy reminded everyone of Dr. Fennigan's suggestion. They helped me to sit down on the bottom step. Daddy and Amma held my leg and lifted it up and down according to my position. Anna and Anil were by my side helping and supporting me to lift me up onto the next upper step. The first few steps were strenuous. Then I got the hang of it. It was a long process and everyone was exhausted. I increased my pace and Daddy tried to scoot up from my back. Then came my snappy reaction, "Don't drag me. It will ruin my jacket." No one said a word.

Later Daddy expressed it humorously, "It was such a strenuous process for everyone, on the stairs, in that cold weather, for that long. In the midst of all this, is it a thing to worry about your jacket getting dirty or worn?" I joined in as he laughed and had fun. I guess I am just that way with certain things—even today.

It was a daylong ordeal for the whole family.

Finally, I made it up through all the stairs; once I got up, the next challenge was getting to use crutches. I just didn't know how to use them initially. It was laborious. Later Anil bought a walker to see if was easier. I was a bit reluctant

My Brush with Death

to try again with this one, but it finally became easier than using crutches at that point in time.

Using this additional support, was putting much stress on my already weakened hands and neck. The first few days I was in lots of pain from the operated area. The slightest shift of that leg position was strenuous—think of sitting down, getting up, going to bathroom, and then having baths from the second day! All these activities were not easy, even before the surgery. Now each of these steps had become arduous. It took the effort of all the five family members' (Amma, Daddy, Anna, Vasavi, Anil) and many accommodating ideas like: Vadina slid a blanket underneath my leg and level it according to my body position when getting off or getting onto the bed; for showers—bringing me into the bathroom in a rolling chair and then putting on a wooden swivel chair and turning it gently to put my legs into the tub. Now I wonder how anyone in this kind of situation manages. I am so fortunate to have my entire family's help, support, and thoughtfulness.

I was glad I had a blood transfusion not too long ago, and we could temporarily avoid the trips to doctor's clinic. The first move outside home was two weeks later for the follow-up appointment. It took lot of planning and extra time to walk down the stairs with crutches. Daddy and Anil were by me on both sides. It was taxing and tiring. Now my heart reaches out to those who use crutches.

Fortunately my surgical area healed normally. Dr. Fennigan recommended physical therapy, to get the strength back to my right leg. I was on crutches for about eight weeks. This period of time was physically the most wearisome.

Fourth Transfusion

The pathology report of the scoop of marrow taken from the orthopedic surgery was in consensus with the MRI and bone scan reports that 80 percent of my marrow had scar tissue. No harmful cells have been found, but what was causing this scar tissue?

My siblings were tested for a bone marrow transplant match. A kit was sent to Akka in Oman. Since my Anna is local, they took his blood sample in the clinic. Anna's matched!

My pathology reports were sent to the Mayo Clinic—still no diagnosis.

My doctor checked for sickle-cell anemia, autoimmune disorders ... I was even sent to a rheumatologist. Dr. Collins sent me to his guru, Dr. Stone. It was a puzzling problem to all the doctors who had seen me. This kind of bone marrow disorder was an uncommon condition for a young 26-year-old, and the unknown cause was even more atypical.

My doctor called in mid-December to keep me posted of his progress with my diagnosis. He did everything he could think of, but no tests gave an answer for the cause of the scar tissue. I could sense his disappointment. Indeed, he took my case as a challenge and worked on it very diligently. I expressed that we are willing to even visit any other doctors or hospitals he could recommend within the country, but ultimately, I would like to him to be my doctor. He worked with so much perseverance and diligence on my case; we have great reverence for all that he did for me. He asked for time to research and said he would get back to me with recommendations.

It was a time of hopelessness. We had been very optimistic until that point, but with the time delay of each test and the frustration of not knowing the root cause of my symptoms, we wondered and worried. How could a perfectly normal 26-year-old with literally no risk factors have a medical condition so puzzling to the doctors?

It had been a long four months since we came to know there was something wrong with my blood creation process.

My Brush with Death

Knowing there was no cancer was a relief in one way, but we were left with agonizing tension—would I ever be healthy again?

I went to bed at night with nagging thoughts, knowing there was something fundamentally not normal with my body. But what? For most diseases including cancer there are approximate healing times and ways to manage the disease. But without a diagnosis, there was no treatment to help me get better.

The other day an elderly gentleman about 75 years old saw Dad taking me in a wheelchair and asked, with a compassionate expression, "What's happened to this young girl?" After listening to what Dad said, he took a rosary with yellow beads out of his pocket, handed it to Dad and said, "Have it with you. She will be alright." Somehow we believed again that God came to us and said these words through him.

My blood levels were going down slowly and progressively—temporarily sustained by blood transfusions. Phone calls and inquiries came from relatives and friends checking on me, asking about the diagnosis, and that added to our feelings of anxiety.

Though we were keeping up our hope and faith in my recovery, still the uncertainty of the future made us secretly ask if I would ever be able to live a normal life, or would I live with this unknown disease. Or would it deteriorate leading to my death? This prolonged period of uncertainty used to pump up my anxiety, create cold sweats and restlessness.

Everyone who knew me was concerned and was praying for me. The only way we kept going then was by enhancing our faith in God. I am blessed to be surrounded with a great family who hid their anxiety with this uncertainty, and fostered hope, faith and encouragement.

My doctor called me back and suggested visiting Dr. Gilbert, a myelofibrosis specialist, in New York City.

Butterfly

We couldn't get an appointment until mid-February with Dr. Gilbert, which worked in my favor, as it was too strenuous for me to travel while on crutches. Also, we contacted Dr. Armugam, another myelofibrosis specialist who was working in Australia at that time. He was of Indian origin and thought he could help with the diagnosis. Graciously he agreed to discuss my situation with my doctor.

I won't forget my fourth transfusion and also my appointment with the rheumatologist.

The night before my fourth transfusion I asked Anil, "Would you please stay with me until the process is initiated? I feel a little nervous when they poke me with those needles, trying to find a good vein. I know your time is important, and preparing for your job interview is crucial. You anyway come to drop us off, and it just takes 20 more minutes."

I slept with much comfort that night as I had expressed my wishes to Anil and made this request. He was with me in the hospital for the first two transfusions, the first one in New Jersey, and the second one at UTSW, Dallas. The next morning Anil drove us to the hospital and dropped Daddy and me at the main entrance. He usually parks the car and comes back. Normally he catches up with us by the time Daddy finds a wheelchair and takes me to the clinic. This time Anil didn't catch up with us. And in the end never came to my procedure. After the whole process was done in the afternoon, I called him and he came to pick us up.

I was upset. I didn't talk much. I was still waiting to see if he realized my mood and would express a word. Nothing came out of him.

Remember the saying, don't go to bed angry? Before going to sleep, I asked him why he didn't stay with me for the process. Again nothing came out of his mouth. "I want you to speak out. I have no idea what is going in your mind if you don't talk. I want to hear you," I said, and I burst into

My Brush with Death

tears. He took me to bed and I felt a little pacified, yet I was still waiting for him to talk to me and express his thoughts. He never did, and that day remained as a hurting memory to me. I recall many times when I was hurt by him for his silence and his actions.

On a cold January day, I went to a different clinic for my rheumatology appointment. Anil drove me, and Daddy was with us. I was still using crutches then. Anil didn't stop by the front entrance of the clinic; rather, he drove to the parking lot which meant we had to walk some distance. I didn't say anything but managed to get out of the car and start walking. I was very hurt and upset—though I still didn't steam out. To forget things is normal. But to watch a loved one walking with crutches in the cold, while she is so weak, when there was a possibility to drop her off at a much closer place was unbelievable. What does this indicate?

Though I am filled with infinite blessings, and all the support and help anyone could possibly have, and many things fell in place and aligned naturally, I still held onto so much pain inside with the uncaring expressions of Anil. Is the mental pain really needed? When my doctor was working relentlessly to heal my illness and my family was working so hard to keep me physically and emotionally strong, it just seemed so unworthy for me to invest my energy in hurts and pain unrelated to my illness.

I don't feel like carrying that painful baggage. I used to think that it would help me to let go of those hurts and heal myself by sharing with my husband. I wanted him to empathize with my pain with compassionate listening. When I felt loved and cared for by him, without my knowledge I used to bloom and open up with a hope to get healed and become a full person again. But at that moment, I didn't experience it with him.

Anil and I went to New York to see Dr. Gilbert the second week of February. She was an elderly doctor in her 70's.

Soon after seeing me she said, "You don't look like the person with this disease. You have such a pleasant smile." I knew it was a sincere compliment. She did blood work even though she had all my reports sent in from my hospital. I always carried my own copies with me—just in case. This visit was to see me in person more than to look at any tests. I'd already had all the possible tests.

This was a strenuous trip for me because I was getting weaker. My head started reeling with the start of the car engine and continued until the engine was turned off. It was very surprising to see this correlation. We stayed at one of our friend's family member's place in New Jersey, so it was about a two-hour trip to downtown Manhattan to Dr. Gilbert's clinic. We went home the next day.

Physical Therapy

I remember going for physical therapy in February until my actual treatment started. One day I couldn't continue my normal workout. I stopped and said, "I am not able to do this. I'm feeling too weak."

I remember the concerned look on the therapist's face. He told me, "Be attentive to what your body is speaking. I don't want you to stretch yourself." Daddy was by my side. He was listening to it all but didn't say anything. I don't think Daddy was happy with me stopping in the middle. I began to question myself. *Is it just a psychological fear or am I really having no energy to continue? I know I have to stretch myself to some pain and efforts to build the strength back in my leg. There is always a fine balance with everything, right?* I wanted to make sure I was not over-stretching and at the same time stretching to a healthy limit to build strength. But I wasn't quite sure if I was doing that.

It didn't take long to assure me that my feelings of weakness were indeed true. I was called by my nurse to

My Brush with Death

confirm my next blood transfusion date. My first three transfusions were about 40 days apart, but the fourth was in 35 days, and now I was scheduled for this fifth one in 25 days.

Around February 20, I received my fifth blood transfusion. I was getting tired of the process and especially the uncertainty of getting better; when would I be completely normal; and would I be going back to work? Or was that condition a deteriorating process? All these thoughts were emotionally nagging me and at times led to hopeless feelings.

While we were going to the hospital, pointing at the bare trees, Daddy said, "Look at those trees, Aruna. They are looking lifeless with no leaves and no greenery. Keep watching them, and in a few months they are going to turn into lively trees with lots of greenery. And your life will just be similar. You are going to be hale and healthy and much stronger than ever."

The blood transfusion was going as usual. But after two hours, I started to feel drowsy and my eyelids felt heavy. I notice an itchy sensation. *This is different, what is happening to me?* I looked at my body and hives were popping up all over. Daddy immediately called the nurses who rushed in to stop the transfusion. *Now what will I do without the blood transfusion? What will become of me?*

Luckily, my doctor was at the hospital and at that moment came to my side. I remember his promise to me a few days ago. Pulling a note card out of his shirt pocket he turned it around and said, "See, you are the number 1 on my priority list." He repeated the same words today again: "I am working on your case as the highest priority. I will find a solution soon." The conviction in his voice gave me hope.

As the doctor was leaving the room, to my surprise, Anna walked in. I saw the concerned, puzzled look on his face with the nurses and the doctor around. What brought him here to visit me at this moment? Again, "energy travels."

I experienced this many times, especially with Anna. He knows just the right moment I need him.

Happy for the miracle, I asked, "Why did you come here at this time?"

"I am in training today close to this location and thought I could see you during my lunch. Is everything alright?"

As if a sudden wave passed through him, Daddy sat upright with an even more courageous face—exhibiting strength. With a firm, strong voice he said, "It is a good sign, Aruna! Your body is rejecting a transfusion. It is time for your bone marrow to turn healthy and produce your own blood."

I don't think Daddy planned to speak these words or thought them inside his head before talking to me. These words just flowed through him in that moment.

We were waiting to hear what to do next. Soon the head nurse came in and said that they would not transfuse me anymore, and we could go home after being monitored for 30 minutes. In the meantime a blood sample was taken to perform a CBC (Complete Blood Count). My platelet count had been gradually decreasing from 140,000 to 28,000.

In a way, I felt relief that I didn't have to have those vein-seeking, poking needles again. I didn't really worry about my future, and surprisingly I was quite calm and peaceful, though a little startled with the change in what had become a routine procedure for me. I didn't project forward, and maybe my tubelight responses came in handy again.

My doctor called me in three days. He kept his word to make my case a priority. After discussing my case with all the other doctors—Dr. Stone, Dr. Gilbert and Dr. Armugam—they came up with the plan to treat me with a combination of oral medicines, steroids—thalidomide, prednisone and tuberculosis antibiotics. He promised to continue to monitor me closely with periodic blood work.

My Brush with Death

And then it happened. My blood counts, which were gradually dropping, *stopped dropping* within a few days. In a couple of weeks, the blood counts all started soaring. Just as my father said earlier, my blood count levels started soaring as the spring started blooming. A real miracle!

No more blood transfusions—just oral pills. The side effects were not really severe—mainly weight gain and physical weakness. However, these side effects are so minor when compared to being near death and now back to life. I am blessed with a miraculous second life.

I was still using my medication and under the supervision of my doctor. My visits to the doctor and blood work decreased gradually, from weekly to bi-weekly to monthly. My medication dosage has gradually been tapered also.

Anil got a job in Little Rock, Arkansas, at the end of April 2001. He moved there and commuted to Dallas every two weeks. By the end of July 2001, my blood count is almost back to normal. Apart from the few side effects, I was recovering. Gradually, I was able to take care of my personal needs. I was even able to walk up and down the stairs and go for short walks with my parents—all small things I took for granted before becoming ill.

After making sure my counts were normal and stable, and seeing my healthy progression, my parents planned their return trip. It had been an extremely long stay for them. They were in a foreign country with vast differences in living style, extreme cold temperatures and not being able to get around by themselves like they do back home. They stayed with the sole and pure intention of taking care of me until I was well again.

Daddy wanted to visit my doctor and his family to personally express our thankfulness and gratitude before they went back home. Amma, Daddy, Anna and I visited him on a Sunday afternoon. We all had a pleasant time together that afternoon, celebrating my recovery.

BUTTERFLY

This is when Dad told me, "You were almost at the gates of death. It is just God who got you back into this world. I am not worried about you anymore." Indeed it was God who brought me back into this world. He served me through my family and my doctor. He blessed me with a second life!

My parents stayed with me until that August. Daddy slowly prepared me to exercise by myself with walks by myself and to get comfortable driving again. It was exactly a year since I last drove a car. What a year—almost like being in a healing cocoon! It was a bit overwhelming, but with Daddy by my side, I gathered enough confidence to get back to my independence quickly. Daddy also encouraged me to read a book with inspirational thoughts—*Tough Times Never Last, But Tough People Do* by Dr. Robert Schuller. He read it regularly and encouraged me to do the same. I planned to keep it on my shelf to read at another time.

It was a quiet day when my parents left for India on August 9. The next day, I was pushed by an unseen force to pick up the book Daddy left with me. I started reading. I not only got hooked on it, but it paved the way for me to become an avid reader. This is the first inspirational book, and the first book I've ever read apart from academic or career related books. Since this book had such a remarkable effect on me, years later, I named my blog after it. My blog url is: Blog.ToughTimesNeverLast.com.

As I pay attention to the diagnosis, "idiopathic myelofibrosis", and its meaning, "unknown scar tissue in the bone marrow (heart of blood cell creation)," and how it affected my life, these words flowed through me.

> It's not something I can forget,
> It wasn't something pleasant to live with,
> There were times of shock, scare, pain within our whole family,

My Brush with Death

But we came out even stronger, bonding even more closely and dearly.
I don't know the reason it happened,
But, it blessed me with a more powerful, meaningful life!
There were times of anxiety and anxiousness, times of hopelessness.
Times of confusion and silent tears.
But now all that counts to me is the greater good it brought.
The miraculous recovery I am blessed with,
The journey to a second life, a more purposeful life!
The wonderful people I met, especially my doctor,
Many nurses who gave hope and comfort with their patience, endurance and their uplifting smiles,
Many thoughts and prayers from all my near and dear ones,
The greater strength and endurance it built in me both physically and emotionally,
Greater faith in God.
Many opportunities to experience and feel the higher consciousness so vividly,
To have strong faith that no matter how tough and hopeless the situation is,
Tough Times Do Not Last, But Tough People Do
Life is Not Always Fair, But God is Always Good
Thank you, Dr. Schuller, for these two powerful books.
I witnessed in my own life,
There is always a bright light at the end of the tunnel.
There is always a greater good out of any situation and circumstance.
Only because of what I went through, I am what I am today.
I am more happy and content with what I am today.
It gave me the experience to connect and relate to others in a much better way.

I get to understand, see through and empathize with the pain and challenges others go through in a much better way.
Thank you, Lord, for giving me many wonderful blessings, Bigger hope and higher faith in You.
And to make me experience that life can be lived in a more beautiful, fuller, richer and exhilarating way through this experience.
I am a better person today!

And so after a year of hospitals, doctors and reports, I was not only well, I was a better person than before. After I was finished with all of my medication, and with my doctor's permission, I joined Anil in Little Rock near the end of 2001. I wanted a new and revitalized relationship with the man I loved. I had no idea that my journey from my cocoon would lead me to another life-changing experience.

Part 2:
My Marriage

Part 2
My Marriage

We were both happy when I joined Anil in Little Rock at the end of 2001. I was relieved that I could take care of my personal needs and get back to myself; he was happy that the strenuous drives to Dallas were over.

We were able to do things together—run errands, cook special foods, visit scenic places. It was fine for a while, but soon, I sensed that we were disconnected in some ways. We had different tastes in entertainment, as he was big on TV, news and movies. I would sit for a bit but realized I could never get into what he was watching, so I began to read. I enjoyed happy and inspiring movies instead of the ones he liked.

Communication with each other was limited to topics like news or his work—dry topics to me. When we went out, he preferred to be quiet and expected me to enjoy the quietness. Indeed, silence is good, but I wanted conversation. I wanted to chat about my day or what I read, but one look at his cold eyes told me to be quiet too. It was not a very happy way to live; I felt upset, let down and alone.

How did I get into such a marriage in the first place?

I was living with my brother's family when I first met Anil on April 11, 1998. He came from New Jersey to Dallas to see me. My parents were also there, visiting us from India. Was this an arranged marriage or a love marriage? Both and neither.

Butterfly

A traditionally arranged Indian marriage of those days was a way for parents to find marriage alliances for their daughter or son. The marriage process usually begins with the realization in the family that their girl is old enough to marry, and for boy after he is settled comfortably with a decent job and earnings. Finding a suitable partner for their girl or boy begins by making inquiries through friends, relatives or a pellilla perayya—a marriage mediator. The parents learn the details about each family, and especially the girl and the boy, to make sure both families have some compatible qualities, keeping in view their general interests, attitudes and natures.

It starts with the pelli chupulu, the bride-seeing ceremony. A group of four to ten people from each family come together for this ceremony. It is usually arranged at the girl's home. The girl is dressed up in traditional dress, a sari, with some auspicious colors, like a yellow-red combination, hair braided, and a garland of flowers tucked into the hair to hang evenly on both sides of the braid, with matching jewelry—necklace, earrings and bangles.

Once the boy's family comes in and settles down, the girl is sent with a tray full of coffee cups to serve the boy and his family. That is the most typical scene when boy and girl get to glance into each other's faces, if they are not shy.

After the girl leaves, the boy's mother, sisters or aunts fill the boy's ears with questions: How is the girl? Did you like her? Depending on this young man's expressions and answers, the ladies of the house probe the girl to see how she talks and how her voice is by asking her to sing. They check for any physical disabilities by asking her to bring something and then watch how she walks.

The boy is interrogated too about his career, typical lifestyle and friends by some of the men from the girl's family—either her elder brothers or dad or uncles. Many eyes observe and follow both the girl and the boy to get an idea of their

My Marriage

behaviors and attitudes. The girl's family is more interested in how settled the boy is in his career, how much money he makes, how stable he is, the comfort level of his lifestyle and a general acceptance of the whole family. They want to assess if their girl will be happy and will be showered with good care and affection in this family. The boy's family checks for how easy the girl gets along with others and how easily she can pick up the skills and accommodations needed in a family setup.

If both parties are okay with what they see, and are still interested, they might let the boy talk to the girl alone for a few minutes—escorted by someone, like a much younger girl or boy, typically less than 10 years old, who wouldn't really understand what was being talked about.

In some segments of the population, parents of both the parties match the astrological horoscopes of their girl and the boy to check their compatibility. Since there is no opportunity for the boy and the girl to date or know each other before the parents give their consent, they are expected to develop a bonding after they are united in the relationship.

In a love marriage, the relationship starts from the mutual interest of the boy and girl. Typically they get to know each other in school/college or maybe they live in the same neighborhood. The attraction comes when the boy and girl get to know each other, finding commonalities or complementary qualities they feel would be nice to have in a married relationship. In a love marriage, if the girl and boy are lucky enough, consent and approval come from the parents and the marriage is celebrated in as much grandeur as a traditional marriage. In some love marriages though, parents disapprove initially and are angry. Yet, they get along later as they don't want to lose the affections of their children and also know that their child, especially the girl, needs their support in many ways after she is married. In a very few cases, parents never accept the marriage happily.

Butterfly

With changing times and with girls studying and working almost as much as boys, parents are more at ease with love marriages, giving consent to their children's opinions. They feel it is better for their child to be married to someone they know well and to their liking rather than someone whom they don't know well.

In my case, the initial contact happened through a mediator. Both fathers had a brief conversation and arranged for Anil to meet me in my family setting. After we met with my brother's family, with my parents present, he expressed an interest and wanted to talk to me personally. We got to meet and talk to each other for a few hours. He was the very first boy I met personally in this kind of setting—each intending to marry. Naturally, there were some nerves as well as excited emotions in me. I did notice some of the clumsy things he did, like not being mindful of spilling his food on the couch. I didn't perceive him as a soft-natured, modest gentleman. I thought he was a bit aggressive, an extroverted person.

After going back to New Jersey he called my brother to express his interest in marrying me, and he wanted to talk to me. I spoke to him for a few minutes. I can't recall now the entire conversation, but he said he was interested in marrying me and asked my opinion. I needed time to think about it.

After hanging up the phone, I spoke to my parents. I did convey that I was interested in marrying him too. Dad asked if I had any strong reasons in wanting to marry him. The two reasons I gave were:

1. He shared that his mom suffered from a psychiatric illness in the past. He didn't have to share it, but by sharing that he made me feel he was a genuine and honest person.
2. I was a relatively timid person. It would be a help to me to have a confident man to lead and help me move forward in life. I thought he was that kind of person.

My Marriage

Amma suggested that we hold off making a decision until they went back to India to meet his family and get more details about him and his family.

More than liking everything about him, I felt committed emotionally. Looking back, I used to ask for advice for very small things, but I made this decision myself. I said firmly in a snappy tone, "I want to marry him, with no further considerations or explanations."

Dad didn't want to say no to me and agreed with my decision. Dad's word was final—so I knew he would not be talked out of supporting my decision.

Anil's family set up the approximate date for the wedding to be in February 1999, which was nine months later. We agreed and began making wedding plans.

Because he was working in New Jersey and I was in Dallas, we got to know each other over our frequent phone conversations. Of course, I was the most talkative. I am not gregarious or extroverted, but the few with whom I open up become victims of my unstoppable A to Z talks. I told him that I have a need to confide myself fully with no restrictions to at least one person. He assured me it was not a problem for him to listen.

I used to talk at length, and he never once asked me to stop. With some laughs and a few interjections in between, I felt he enjoyed my conversation, so I would speak with even greater enthusiasm. As long as I shared and he listened—and answered my specific questions—my needs were filled and I was happy.

It didn't take long for me to learn that he was a foodie, sings well and mimics the way people speak. I was even more attracted to him and asked him to sing and imitate various people. I don't have these skills, but I enjoyed listening to his songs and how he spoke. That's when I developed an interest in cooking and kept an eye open for good recipes.

BUTTERFLY

Until then I didn't cook much. Soon I had a collection of recipes and nice songs.

Our engagement date was set for January 18, 1999, and our wedding on February 7. The engagement was a formal ceremony before marriage to exchange rings and get together with family and friends. Both of the ceremonies took place in India because that is where most of our family members reside. We flew separately to India but would both return together to New Jersey to live.

I looked forward to spending time with my parents before our wedding. I was happy and excited just as any other girl getting married. My parents celebrated both the engagement and wedding ceremonies in a very grand way—with the best they could financially afford.

There is a famous Telugu song, "Aha Na Pelli Anta!" ("Aha/Wow, It's My Wedding!", "aha" is an exclamatory word similar to what it says in English; "na" means my/mine; "pelli" means wedding; and "anta", seems. So the meaning of the phrase is "It's my wedding!") It is sung in a happy, joyous tone. It was that moment in my life. It was my wedding! I was filled with dreams of a wedding day with the two lovebirds' story lasting forever after. For the first time, without Amma insisting, I was taking good care of my body with hour-long baths, massaging my skin with oil. My cousins and aunts teased me about the glow in my face and shiny skin.

As the wedding day approached, the house was getting filled with relatives and neighbors checking in. I was showing off all the colorful saris, jewelry and bangles. Amma and I finished the major shopping for saris within the first few days of my arrival in India. It takes a long time for all the stitching that goes into wearing a sari—getting blouses custom stitched by the tailor. Saris need falls to be stitched and the edges hemmed; with the dozens of saris needed and all the tailoring work that goes into them, it takes a few weeks to

My Marriage

have them done well. Amma had already reserved the tailor's time months in advance. "When my girl arrives from America, we will have dozens of blouses and saris to stitch. They have to be made really well. The bride's saris are the first priority. As soon as you complete them, we want my pedda ammayi's (elder daughter's), my kodalu's (daughter-in-law's) and my manavaraalu's (granddaughter's) done."

Anyone approaching the street could figure out there was a wedding going on in this house from the shamiana (wedding tent) and the decorations with lights similar to lights during the Christmas season. All the door entrances are decorated with mamidakulu (mango leaves) and puvvulu (flowers) in rich colors.

For our engagement ceremony Amma called in a beautician from the parlor to do my makeup. I wasn't pleased at all; I thought I looked almost like a buffoon with a painted face. I wondered why people go to beauty parlors, as I have never been to a beauty parlor in my life until then. I feel I have natural beauty and don't need to go to the beauty parlor.

With this experience, I did my own makeup to my taste—like Goldilock's phrase, not too much, nor too little, but just right—for my wedding day. Of course I had all the help I wanted with my Akka and Vadina around me, and they validated that I had the perfect look.

Apart from taking care of my own makeup, I let my pinnilu (Mom's sisters) do the rest: pleat my sari, do the poola jada (long hair plait decorated with flowers) and put the special kalyana thilakam (special wedding bindi), and put on all my jewelry, including a handful of red and green bangles. All this took over an hour with the help of many hands. Yet, it was exciting. It was my wedding!

I was dressed up in my perfectly gorgeous outfit—a purple and pink pattu (silk) sari with golden colored checkers and small flowers. I was feeling proud, like the queen of the day. Of course it is my wedding, and I *am* the bride. I stopped in front of the mirror one last time to make sure my makeup, hair, accessories and everything about my appearance was not even an itsy-bitsy bit less than perfect.

Turning to my cousins, I asked, "How do I look?"

A big, beautiful, gorgeous "so pretty" was their answer.

Then we went to the marriage hall with my parents and siblings surrounding me. The wedding hall and the mandapam (wedding stage) were beautifully decorated with a variety of flowers—jasmine, roses, lilies. The smell of jasmine pervades the air. Our wedding was in the evening, and it was already dark. The lit decorations added more brightness and color to the arena.

I, along with my close family members, entered the stage and sat down to one side, while Anil's family sat to the other side. Initially, the bride and groom don't get to see each other as they put out a curtain between the two sides. A poojari (priest) chants some spiritual marriage mantras and asks the bride and groom and their parents to repeat some of them. I had no idea what all of them meant but just repeated them after the priest in the best way I could.

The main part of this process was jilakara-bellam, where the bride and groom put a piece of mould made from jaggery-cumin on each other's heads, and the priest chants the marriage vows mantras. This takes place at the set muhurtham time. Now the curtain between the bride and groom is removed. Anil and I got to exchange a quick glance at each other for the first time during the wedding ceremony. All the guests came and blessed us by putting akshinthalu (rice mixed with auspicious turmeric, vermilion powder and flower petals) on our heads.

This is followed by tying the mangalasutra (two gold discs, one from each parent's family, looped through a pasupu thadu-yellow thread) with moodu-mudulu (three knots), which

My Marriage

represents the physical, mental and spiritual union of the couple.

Now we changed our dresses from traditional to the relaxed white dresses, which are symbols of auspiciousness and serenity. I changed to a white sari with a maroon border, which I love.

Then we could enjoy the fun part of the wedding, pouring thalambralu on each other's heads and also getting rings from a pot. It's a fun way to check who leads, the bride or the groom. I think Anil won this game.

Then each of the relatives and friends approached us for a brief minute to introduce themselves and offer their gifts. We conveyed our gratitude for their presence and blessings. It was a night of celebration and special magic—after all, "aha na pelli anta!"

After the wedding, we traveled a bit, and in a few days everyone departed for home and the house was quiet and empty.

When we were at my parents' home, for the first time Anil seemed quiet and detached. It seemed as if all his bubbliness and zesty nature faded away. I had no idea why he was so. I asked gently, "What happened, Anil? You are looking faded. Is everything okay?" He just rolled his eyes with no answer. I asked excitedly, "Shall we go out and buy some sweets?"

He answered, "No. I don't want to go. You can go if you want." Still there is not much cheer in his face.

"Did I upset you, Anil?"

"No."

I began to feel a little nervous and wondered what happened. When we came back to his parents' place, he was much more relaxed and so was I.

We returned to New Jersey on Friday night, so we had the weekend to settle down and do some essential shopping before the week commenced. Anil was working in New York City, so he had a long work commute from New Jersey by train. At least our apartment was within walking distance from the train station. Normally he left home at 6:45 a.m. and came back exhausted at 6:30 p.m.

After his return, having dinner, watching TV, it was time to sleep. During weekends we had time to watch an extra movie, catch up with friends and family over the phone, shop for groceries and occasionally go out to a restaurant, a park or a museum. Once a month he worked on Saturday. His work was stressful, so he did not want to talk much. He wanted to be quiet.

I convinced myself, *Okay, he is quiet because he is so stressed with his long work hours. This will pass soon, and we will spend more time interacting with each other. I need to have more openness and patience.* Inside I wished he would talk about his work stress, so that I could help him feel lightened and hear what was on his mind.

Because I didn't work, I used my time to cook what he liked for dinner and even made something for his lunch. He liked what I cooked, and I was happy to cook to his tastes.

After seven months of being married, I got a job with a long commute of 70 miles each way. Working on the new job skills and trying to cope with my work was a bit challenging. My workload wasn't too heavy, but my lack of experience in using my job skills put pressure on me. Sometimes I worked 12 to 16 hours a day. Our roles switched. My husband cooked our dinner sometimes, and on a few occasions he even packed my lunches in the morning. I was very thankful to him for him doing it and I felt bad that I didn't have time for taking care of cooking at home.

Thankfully, after two months, we moved to a new apartment, which was much closer to work. That helped so much in cutting down the drive time. My long working hours continued until April, when I began to work only eight to ten hours a day.

Even though I was coming home earlier, I didn't have much interest in cooking or in taking care of housework. I began to feel as if I was suffocating—a reeling sensation especially while I was in the kitchen. It could have been poor ventilation in the small kitchen. I'm not sure what it was and at times I wondered if I was being lazy.

In May 2000, my parents came for a visit on their way to my brother's home in Dallas. I was surprised to hear Anil complain about me: "She doesn't cook even one day. She asks me to take this vacation, that vacation. We eat the same food for days from refrigerator."

They were heartrending complaints, and inside my head I thought, *What happened to all the effort I put in cooking the dinners and packing his lunches for the first seven months of our marriage? Where were his compliments that I cook delicious food, that I put my heart into doing what he likes? Were they false words? I was working 16-hour days when he cooked our dinners or packed my lunch box. Did he do it out of care and concern? What about the loving, kind and thoughtfulness I thought he showered on me? Were the nice, loving compliments he said just sugarcoated falsehoods?*

I was broken. *Why did he call me sweet names? I prefer bitter truth over sugarcoated untruth. Or did he lack the courage and openness to express his hurts to me?*

I didn't know why he needed to talk this way to my parents. They were visiting us for the first time after more than a year, all the way from India. They would be leaving in two days. If he was unhappy with me about something, he could have communicated with me about it.

I was hurt and sad for his bitter remarks about me, as well as for creating an unhappy scene for my parents. The house was quiet. Finally, before my parents were leaving, he said

BUTTERFLY

to them, "I am sorry for whatever happened. You are like my mom and dad; I don't want to hurt you. Please forget what happened." Dad and Mom cheered up and left for Dallas in a better mood.

In a few weeks, we planned a trip to India for Anil's younger brother's wedding. Anil wanted to take a break from his work, upgrade his skills and find a new job. With his brother's wedding date fixed in August, he wanted to continue in his current job until after our India trip.

We boarded for our India trip on August 4. It was a long 24-hour journey, and I noticed my legs were swollen. Though I've never had this kind of problem before in any of my previous flights, I wasn't alarmed because I noticed swollen feet in my dad and also my sister during long flights.

My swollen feet didn't really bother me as much as the urinary incontinence I was experiencing even before the travel. I was concerned about it for the long flight, as well as all the travel we would be doing in India. I expressed this concern to my husband, who said he would be checking on me and would be offering help—not to worry.

I wish my parents had been in India, but they were not. Neither of our parents' places have airports, so it was another nine-hour car trip to my in-laws' home. In between we made a quick day-stop to see all my aunts, uncles and grandma. All gathered to see us in a happy reunion.

Finally, we reached my in-laws' house. My mother-in-law looked at me in a cross way, but I didn't know why. She made me nervous. Anil did not say anything. This felt like putting a pinch of salt on the wound. I was feeling dizzy and feeling the sensation that I might fall while walking down the stairs. I asked my husband to please stay by me. But the next time we were walking at the train station, I got dizzy and began to sweat. Everyone was in their own hurry. I felt scared and alone with no one by my side in that moment.

My Marriage

A few who knew me could see that I was not well, and they expressed this in front of my husband who seemed insulted. I really didn't worry or think anything was wrong with my health, but I was going through emotional stress. I continued to be fearful of my mother-in-law's unusual behavior, and my husband's coldness threw me off.

The next morning Anil asked me to get ready to see a doctor. As we were almost ready to leave, my father-in-law interrupted and said, "Why are you guys rushing to see a doctor? She will be fine if she eats a piece of jaggery." Anil quieted his father and we went to the hospital to see a doctor.

The doctor performed a CBC (complete blood count) and other tests. He prescribed some medication to give me relief. When we returned home, my feet were still swollen. That was the beginning of my health and my relationship challenges.

Coping at Home

With a husband that did not share my interests, I had to find ways to divert my mind to something to keep me happy. Since we didn't have many interests to mutually share, I started finding ways to divert my mind to something constructive. I got passionately involved in reading. Books and journaling became my good companions. In fact, I craved reading and journaling. Reading kept me up and inspired; writing—mostly journaling—helped me to vent and make myself clear on my life.

I am grateful to Anil for many reasons. One day he told me about a group called Toastmasters that was dedicated to improving public speaking skills. Somehow I got fascinated. I knew I was terrible at public speaking and needed to improve on it, and this would be of help anywhere—at work, talking to strangers or building a social network. It would be especially helpful because English was not my mother tongue; I was not at ease in communicating, especially to those who do not speak Telugu, my mother tongue.

We soon joined Toastmasters together. He attended a few meetings, did a few speeches and then quit. For me it was a new experience, and very intimidating in the beginning. However, I persisted. Though I had a long gap in membership because of my health, when I got back into it, I was a more active and passionate member. I love Toastmasters! It helped me transform from a shy, timid speaker to one who loves making presentations. And as Toastmasters are fond of saying, I got my butterflies to fly in formation.

Anil is indeed a creative person. He sings and he draws quite well. He gave me good ideas for my speeches, as well as creative ideas for decorating the house and for my craftwork. I will always be thankful to him for the ideas he gave me. And I'm happy I took advantage of them with my strength, diligent work, quick action and ability to persist.

I probably even learned to sing because of him. He sings very well and sparked my interest in wanting to learn to sing. I didn't have the singing skills, nor am I a spontaneous singer, yet I learned the hard way by writing down lyrics, memorizing and practicing again and again. I am still not a great singer, but I am happy that I can please myself and satisfy my inner desire to sing. I even got to fulfill my desire to improve my drawing skills by learning to paint in a five-week oil painting course. Having these kinds of experiences adds an extra dimension to us and to our way of communicative expressions.

I looked forward to having fun with his creative interests and asked him to play games with singing or draw something together. Most of the time he showed no interest in a game when I asked, but sometimes we'd play a few minutes, and then he'd say, "Later."

We seemed to be diametrically opposite in the sense that when I am involved in something, I do it passionately,

My Marriage

persistently and become unstoppable. His way is to have a brief experience with many things but not become involved in anything for long.

As the years progressed, to some extent I got used to fulfilling my wants and needs for myself instead of holding on to my initial expectations about a marriage filled with mutual discussions of issues, doing things together and the kind of sharing that enhances joys and lessens sorrows. We were like two single people living under the same roof.

I wanted to have children, but he always put me off by saying he didn't want to stress me because of the health issues I went through. Every time I expressed my interest, his response was cold. I wished he were open in sharing what was on his mind.

When someone asked about when we would have children, he'd say, "I like kids. But since Aruna went through so much in the past with her health issues, I don't want to stress her." These words gave me an impression he was forgoing his desire to have kids because of my health condition.

I had a keen interest in becoming a mom, and I knew I could do what was required of a mom. I felt I was ready. I worked hard to lose the extra 25 pounds gained due to my medication and got back to physical fitness. I was back to work, taking care of myself and the household activities. Of course I would need his support and help as it takes both parents' responsibility and commitment to raise children. And if he were really concerned about me, why didn't he assure me? He could have said, "Aruna, don't worry. I will extend you all the help and support you need for us to raise our children." It was not something I could ask him but silently wished for.

I needed his acceptance and willingness to go for it. He didn't hear me, which made me feel helpless, suppressed and even depressed. I knew the decision needed to come from both parents in a loving way.

I turned to my friend, my journal. I recorded this entry on September 17, 2007, which, for the first time, encouraged me. The words were from a law of attraction book: "I can get anything I want, if my want is strong and I create great feelings for it."

These thoughts inspired me to dream of my child. I used to vividly visualize every detail of the baby, of me experiencing the baby, and lived in those feelings. I journaled every detail and all the feelings I had. I started giving greater and greater attention and focus and started feeling so good and wonderful, which was an indication that I was going to manifest and receive my want of becoming a mom very soon.

My husband, by himself, expressed his interest in having a child. He said, "I am not able to say no to you any more, looking at you and your fervid expressions."

This was one big step towards my manifestation!

This is the result of the law of attraction. I can manifest anything I want if I generate those intense emotions. The more attention and emotion I give, the quicker I attract. I am attracting such beautiful things so quickly. Of course, I now believe I am driven by a higher consciousness to generate these intense emotions.

In no time, I conceived and carried my precious one.

Anil was out of a job for two months. Then he got a job offer in a different city, but he wasn't very keen on leaving me. I assured him I was doing well and encouraged him to go for it. While I was in my sixth month of pregnancy, he quit his job saying he wanted to be there to take care of me. I pleaded with him not to quit his job, and if I really need help I would let him know—then he could quit. Also, I knew my parents were coming from India to help me during my delivery.

But he did quit his job and came back home. We had a good time for a few days. Soon the reality of the past set in

My Marriage

and he went back to his normal ways—not talking much and looking stressed and gloomy.

He said he was stressed because he did not have a job, yet he chose to quit his job.

I still attended some parties by myself—graduation parties, baby shower parties. He chose not to come to my own baby shower at my work, yet he told me he quit his job to take care of me.

Finally, the arrival of our miracle baby! We named him Keshav.

Anil was with me through my entire labor. After bringing the baby to us, we had pictures taken with the doctor and nurse crew and everyone departed. Oh, soon after the delivery, I had an itchy sensation all over my body and I was given Benadryl. My eyes were getting heavy and I was about ready to fall asleep. I looked for Anil to come and talk to me or just be with me to share a glance at each other in that moment. He was sitting at the other end of the wide long room with his head down. *Please look at me, I am just across from you*, I was saying inside, looking at him. Just a head lift and a look at my face and he could tell I was looking for him. Thirty minutes passed, but he never looked my way.

Then the nurses came to help me move to another room, and I asked for their help to go to the bathroom. That's when I burst into uncontrollable tears and the nurses worried that I was in pain. I just couldn't talk. Finally, I managed to tell them that I was not in any pain and just felt very emotional. I didn't cry or even scream much during my entire labor, and the nurses and doctor were surprised that I took pain very well.

But now I was broken emotionally as I missed him being by my side in that moment. Finally, I cheered myself up and felt better. Still, I waited for him to come and talk to me. I thought he would come and stop by me at least before he went to sleep.

I kept waiting, controlling my sleep until he fell asleep and I heard his snoring. Surely it was a long day for him.

My parents came to help me out and I was happily enjoying my little one. I started back to work after taking off for a six-week maternity leave. It was all good except to see Anil's hesitation and discomfort around my parents in our own house. I wished he was comfortable and at ease with them. Fortunately, I am blessed with wonderful parents who didn't let this pull them down or force them to give up their intended purpose.

Anil started working in the middle of October after being out of a job for over six months. We took turns waking up during the night to attend to the baby's needs. When my son was four months old, my parents went back home and I found a sitter to take care of my son during the day; she was a very nice, warm lady.

We established a routine: Anil took the baby to the sitter in the morning before he went to work, and I picked him up in the evening. By the time Anil came home, I finished giving Keshav a bath, fed him and finished my cooking and small chores.

Our lives changed the Monday after that Thanksgiving.

I picked up Keshav in the evening, as usual, and came home. I looked at the clock and it was past the time Anil normally comes home. I waited for another 30 minutes and tried calling him but his cell phone was off. I panicked. I knew none of his coworkers because he just recently started working there; all I knew was that it was a small place, and he worked with four others. And then I recalled that one of his colleagues called our home phone the day before Thanksgiving. I dialed that number and spoke with someone; I can't recall the name now. I asked if he had seen Anil. He said the last time he saw Anil was that afternoon around 3:30 p.m. but that he stepped out and didn't see him later.

My Marriage

It was past 7 p.m. so I had no choice but to call 9-1-1. I explained the situation and that I was concerned. The officer said they would come to my home to take the details. As I hung up, the phone rang. It was Anil. I asked where he was and told him I'd just called 9-1-1 because I was worried. So after calling 9-1-1 back to cancel the alert, we spoke by phone.

Anil was in Missouri, the place where he worked while I was pregnant, and was living with his previous roommate. He mentioned he would be working on the current project from that location. He explained that some priest mentioned it would be good for us to live separately and so he was doing just that. I asked why he didn't tell me while he was home and he said, "If I told you, you wouldn't let me go. So I didn't tell you."

I didn't fully comprehend what was going on. But I didn't have time to think as I had to attend to my baby's needs. I made arrangements for the sitter for the next day. I'm very glad that my son's babysitter graciously accepted me leaving him early and assured me it was not a problem.

Anil tried calling a few times, but I just couldn't talk to him. I already had a plateful of things to handle. Until recently, my parents were there taking care of everything for the baby and all chores at home. After my parents left, Anil left me and the baby. Now I was all by myself with my little one. I can understand if he had some problems with me, but how can he get out of the responsibility of taking care of this little child?

After six weeks of staying apart, he called and left a message on the machine informing me that he was leaving for India and wanted to take Keshav with him. I was shocked. He called back and I answered this time. I said that our baby was not a toy to take after being away from him for six weeks. If he wanted to work something out, he could come home and talk. He persisted that he was going to India.

Butterfly

I pleaded with him to come home before going to India, and finally he came. He stayed for three months. Those three months were the most stressful times of all. Since he quit his job, he was home for the most part. He didn't enjoy being with the baby other than a few times here and there—nothing consistent. He was not happy with himself. So gloomy. I was taking care of the baby by myself, dropping him off at the sitter, picking him up, running errands and doing household chores. When I thought about it, it was not much change from the six weeks when he was gone. I thought inside, *Why can't he just be normal? Why can't he enjoy the happy things we are blessed with—if nothing else, enjoy our precious little one?*

I encouraged him not to worry about his job, because I was earning enough for our needs. I wanted him to be stress free. He said he was stressed about not having a job, but I noticed that he's also stressed when he does have a job. Strange. I just didn't understand what he wanted, what his words meant and what his true intentions were.

After three months of this, he suggested, "Let's go back to India this weekend. You go and offer your resignation at work. And we will pack the bags and go home."

"What? What will we do?"

His reply was quick, "Ideally, we will do nothing for six months. We both are stressed and need a break."

"But what about the expenses, and especially of the baby?"

"He is a baby. He doesn't need anything. He will easily survive."

For the first time, I stood strong without falling off to his sweet words.

For the first time also, I considered his patterns. Many times during my pregnancy he talked of fantasies; he wanted to start this business or that business, and he wanted me to

My Marriage

quit my job. I said that I didn't need to quit my job for him to find his dream business, and I can quit after his dreams come true.

His words: "I don't want you to work. Instead, I want you to enjoy being happily at home, and I want to see you happy." At times his words used to tempt me that I should quit my job. Not that I didn't like my job, but I thought that perhaps being home would make him happy.

But I had to come to my senses and hold off my temptation. When I wasn't working, the first seven months after our marriage and all the five years I was on disability, I couldn't make him any happier. Once I got back to work, I was feeling much better that I was doing something worthy and could help him by not financially burdening him, and on top of that, I enjoy my work.

Yet every time he said to quit my job, I went through this process of getting tempted, holding on and thinking through things logically rather than spontaneously getting to this decision. At times I felt bad that I was denying his request, and I used to go back and forth within myself whether or not it was the right thing to do. Sometimes these thoughts continued to confuse and puzzle me for days.

With the ongoing experiences, I couldn't completely trust him and wondered, Did *he really mean what he said?* Frankly, I still do not know which words he really meant and which he didn't mean. It hurts and robs my peace to doubt the words of my own husband. At the same time I was noticing him not keeping the promises he made.

If I had quit my job believing his words while I was pregnant, what would have been the survival state—with both of us not working, having a small baby and all the monthly expenses we incurred?

These thoughts were haunting me. I told him I needed some time to arrange for all things to move, and also that

I might wait to apply for citizenship, which was not too far away. I told him if he wanted to go home to take a break that was fine with me. I told him to come back after he felt he had enough of a break. But he persisted that if he went to India, he would not come back.

The next day he would not eat or get out of bed for the full day. We had dinner the previous night and he went to bed. He didn't get up the next morning when I left with the baby. By the time we returned home, he was still in bed. Normally, he cannot go without eating a single meal, and now he was without food all day. I could neither make him get up nor eat. I didn't know what to do. It was very stressful and alarming. *What if he gets really low in energy and something happens to him?* With the little one needing my attention, this unusual behavior built up more pressure and anxiety. I finally called one of his friends and explained the situation and requested that he and his wife come to our home to make Anil eat. Finally they made him eat.

Then I realized that I had to pleasingly persuade him to go to India even if he persisted he wouldn't come back. I managed to get him to agree to go to India alone though I didn't want to miss him. The most pressing thing at that point was for him to reach his home and his family safely, which he did—in relatively much better energies.

I heard from him every now and again. And then after a couple of months, he called and made a shocking statement, "I think it would be better for us to get separated and divorced."

I was speechless, as I didn't expect it from him.

Getting divorced or being a divorcee is relatively easy to accept nowadays. But this was not the case during my divorce. In the time and environment where I grew up, there was a social stigma around divorce. In our family my divorce would be the first. In fact, when I grew up, I didn't know of

My Marriage

anyone with children raised by a single mom or dad or with step-siblings.

Because I was a go-with-the-flow type of girl who just wanted to be part of the normal crowd, deciding to get a divorce wasn't an easy choice. I may not have had the courage to file myself. If I had, probably I would have made that choice a long time back. I thank God for helping me with Anil initiating the divorce process, whether he really meant to or not.

Today I am glad that I chose divorce. Not that it was the happiest thing, but I am happier today than what I was when I was married. The single thought I attribute to my becoming a stronger person is this phrase: "Accept 100 percent responsibility" for my life and for my son's life.

I tried to be strong, and I felt a lot better as the months progressed. I was lonely, but I was finding myself. If not happy, I was free from the great burden of stress when Anil was around.

I journaled my own thoughts about how we differed in personalities and chemistries:

He needs sympathy to stay low;
I need empathy to grow stronger.
He wants to stay in a low profile;
I want to bring out the best in me.
He dreams and fantasizes, but doesn't take any action—or gives up;
I am not a high-achiever with great skills. I just take action on the very small thing I want to do.
He says "slow down, relax, do nothing, don't overexcite."
I am happy in doing things with gusto. I take quick action and with enthusiasm on the little things I want to learn or do. Acting with gusto gives me drive and encouragement.

His focus is food, and relaxation is movies or staying quiet;
To me, eating good, nutritious food is a basic need for living, and not the purpose of living.
My focus is growth, learning, communication, sharing.
He prefers silence between us;
For me, silence between us is unbearable.

In his eyes, no matter what, it is my fault. Whatever he does or says—it is his choice and right. My right is to make my life happy and free from the many folds of stress. So with regards to his suggestion of divorce I said, "Okay, if this is what you decided, I am okay with it."

Marriage can be the sweetest relationship and the greatest fulfillment to experience. It, however, takes work to nurture, have true commitment, responsibility, open communication and understanding each other to bring out the best in each other and the relationship. But when those elements are missing, and the path and ways can never meet, never bringing out the greater good in each other, it is much better to live separately instead of fighting and expecting the other to change.

If someone outside does a small good deed, it will remain in our hearts as good forever. But ironically, when it comes to life partners, hurts overtake all the goodness, unless efforts are made to heal or at least understand and empathize. It's sad but true. No one can change anyone unless the other person wants to change for themselves.

Our divorce process went very smoothly and quickly as it was with mutual consent. He took care of all of it. I just made sure I understood the legal terminology and signed my consent.

But the day before we filed, he threw me another surprise. He called to say, "Let's drop this filing."

My Marriage

"What?"

"I really didn't mean to go for a divorce. Initially, I thought you would soon be coming back to India. I waited for a few months. Still you didn't come. Then I initiated this so you felt threatened and would either come back to India or would ask me to come back to you."

I felt, for the first time in our married life, that he spoke up and I could clearly and assuredly see his intentions. It helped me to go for our divorce even more assuredly.

He called me a few months after our divorce approval to say he wanted to come back.

I asked why. "I was out of a job then, so couldn't stay."

"Do you have a job now?"

"No, I don't. I don't even want to work. Maybe I will do some odd jobs."

I knew inside my heart that it was not going to be an easy life living with him, with his reluctance to work. If he wasn't working due to health issues or some other problem I would be still doing whatever I could to support him and sustain the family. But it was beyond that, and for reasons unknown to me yet. Though I was a bit emotional, I knew I had to be strong within myself. To answer him I said, "Earlier, I said it was okay for you not to work with the intention of you not to feel pressured and stressed. I wanted to give a helping hand to lift you up. I can't help you when you don't want to work, nor am I in a state to provide you a living."

He revealed a little more as the conversation dragged on. He said he really wanted to be with me and the baby. I was tempted for a bit. But an intuitive voice in my head said not to go back to that miserable life again. I can recall how much responsibility he had for the baby and how much he enjoyed his time with the baby. I am glad I answered with a firm "No."

With a frail voice, he said, "Okay, if this is what you decided, I am okay with it."

Butterfly

If I look back, between the two of us, I was the noisy one, the talker. I was the one rewinding the tapes of my hurts whenever I felt uncared for or un-empathized with. I was the one who used to drag out the conversations with a hope to have a final solution of gaining understanding and empathy. So it is me who was responsible for many sleepless nights.

Now I see it was my expectations which caused my pain, and, of course, pain for him. If I didn't have any expectations, or learned to enjoy my many blessings and let go of the rest, I wouldn't have been hurt. I would have enjoyed the flow of life better as I do now. This is a lesson I learned much later.

The two major events in my life, my illness and my divorce, have brought about in me a transformation.

Though both had impacted me and built my strength, courage and determination in their own ways, I can say that I drastically transformed myself with my divorce, and at a very rapid rate.

During the recovery from my illness, my entire family's unanimous efforts, support, encouragement, responsibility, faith and beliefs blessed me with a second life. With my divorce, I had to consult and seek advice and guidance of many, but it was entirely I who had to make that major final decision and accept total responsibility for my life and that of my little one to move ahead.

Let me take a brief moment here to share my current beliefs regarding marriage. A marriage is a communion of two complete individualized beings from a whole set of individual values, beliefs and backgrounds. It does take a lot of effort and give and take to develop mutual understanding, mutual fulfillment and growth. However, the goal should be to attain mutual fulfillment and growth and have a meaningful purpose.

It's not a matter of who is right or wrong, or who is good or bad, but rather a matter of becoming the person who

My Marriage

will aid, support and contribute to the other person's values and beliefs in a wholehearted, happy way. If so, there is every reason to strive to be in the relationship no matter how many differences and how much effort or how long it takes for one to become that person.

In retrospect, when it doesn't happen, knowing fully that our needs for mutual fulfillment and growth will never be met, and our paths are totally different, parallel and will never coincide, it's so much better to seek separate ways of living instead of expecting from each other what the other person doesn't have and cannot give.

Sometimes two people may not get together in a marriage for neither partner's faults. It is just a matter of not being able to adjust to each other needs and wants. In our case, the paths we both want to move toward are just not compatible and could never coincide. I believe each of us deserves to live happily and to be our best! When it is not possible to live better together, it's so much better to live as individuals rather than building up the negative, draining, drowning energies, lowering the other's best self.

I now completely believe that no one but me was responsible for the way my life was, the way I lived and the way I am living now. It's me who let my life happen the way it happened to me, and now again it's me who is completely responsible for the way I am living now.

One major, significant difference, though, is that until the second major happening in my life, I *let* my life happen to me. From then on, I am *making* my life happen for me. It's a mere one-word difference: letting and making. But this difference turned my life upside down in a very positive, flourishing direction.

No matter what, everyone deserves to live happily and live a life of love, joy and peace. We both deserve much better lives. I have no regrets for what happened because I have

Butterfly

learned many valuable lessons. I am not a perfect person and have my own strengths and weaknesses. But I am glad I became a fuller person—like a butterfly emerging from a cocoon. I am now free—free from expectations, free from fluctuating on how I should be, free from unneeded anxiety. There can be million reasons for a divorce, but a single reason is sufficient to stay together in a relationship. Life is beautiful, and I am ready to live an absolutely gorgeous experience.

Part 3:
Spiritual Transformation

Part 3
Spiritual Transformation

Bhagavad Gita, chapter 6, verse 5

uddhared atmanatmanam
natmanam avasadayet
atmaiva hy atmano bandhur
atmaiva ripur atmanah

Translation:
"One must deliver himself with the help of his mind, and not degrade himself. The mind is the friend of the conditioned soul, and his enemy otherwise."

    Our mind can either be our best friend or our worst enemy depending on what we feed it. An attached mind suffers from bondage, while a detached mind enjoys liberation.

    When I was able to let go of my marriage, I began to learn how to make my life the way I want it to be. I don't have expectations from anyone. If I want something, I accept responsibility and make ways to make it happen. If for some reason I can't make it happen, I realize there is a better way or a better time for it, so I let it go and keep myself open and free. I find good out of every encounter and situation no matter if it is favorable, neutral or unfavorable. Life seems beautiful and is flowing gracefully. All the help I want is sent my way. I feel this is happening almost effortlessly because of the spiritual transformation happening within me.

What is spirituality?

To me, spirituality is faith and belief that we are created and functioning by higher powers. You can call this higher power by the name of your choice: God, The Divinity, The Spirit, The Source or The Super-Soul. No matter which God you believe in or even if you don't believe in God, most people believe in the fact that there exists a super power which created us, the human beings, animals, plants, the earth, the sun, the moon and the stars.

Even if we look at the intricate design of our human bodies—the way each part coordinates and maintains perfect harmony within, the way our hands move, legs move, digestive system works and the way our sensory organs perceive—it is beyond amazing. How about the intellect and creativity of our minds? What about the loving, peaceful being within ourselves? What is the force behind all these super amazing abilities and qualities?

This higher power, the super power behind all this magnificent creation, I will refer to as the Magnificent Source, Source or Divine Spirit from now on. You can think of it as a person, or even a presence, which is all-pervading, eternal, existing around us, above us and within us.

This Magnificent Source is omnipotent, omnipresent and eternal. It's indestructible and has no death. It is kind, compassionate, loving, graceful, abundant, joyful, blissful, forgiving and at peace. There are no specific measurable attributes to this Source. It encompasses and engulfs the entire existence.

We human beings are the most precious, creative, spiritual beings created by the Magnificent Source, and we are part of it. We are a piece of the divine Magnificent Source. We may not be as powerful as the abundant, infinite, eternal

SPIRITUAL TRANSFORMATION

Magnificent Source, but we can experience all the amazing powers of this Magnificent Source by staying connected to it.

I love the metaphor I read in the book *The Shift* by Dr. Wayne Dyer. He compared the Source to the ocean and each of us to a drop of water in the ocean.

The moment we disconnect from the Source, all our magnificent powers start dwindling just like a drop of water loses its power when it is taken out of the ocean. A drop of the ocean has the same composition of the water in the ocean and experiences all the abundance of the ocean when it is part of the ocean. However, when it is taken out of the ocean, the drop loses its connection to the source and soon perishes. Similarly, as long as we stay connected to the Magnificent Source, we can experience all the amazing powers of the Source creation. When we get disconnected from the Magnificent Source, we wither away and do not perform at our best potential.

The Divine Spirit in us has the same composition as the Divine Spirit in the Magnificent Source. This Divine Spirit is present in all of us. It is the common thread holding us together, allowing us to co-create, maintain the beautiful harmony and have absolutely everything we need and want.

When we see ourselves as part of this Magnificent Source, connect and commune with it, we become one with it and experience all the magnificent powers of this creation, without any limitations.

By connecting with our Source, we expand our horizons from our limited self to a bountiful abundance. We don't feel the need to win, to be right and to compete against anyone. We see there is abundance for everyone, and that each of us can have everything we want and need. We live gracefully, at peace and full of love.

When I said that we don't feel the need to win, or compete against anyone, it does not mean that I am suggesting living in apathy or boredom, doing nothing or living in the status-quo. No, I am not. Rather, I mean living the life we want, doing things we love to do and are passionate about for the joy of doing, for the joy of giving, but not for the results or for winning a competition. We live in joy, at peace, with no barriers or limitations.

I also don't mean being irresponsible for one's life, or being inactive. Each of us is indeed called upon to live the life of our purpose and accept 100 percent responsibility for our lives. Living becomes a joy when we learn to co-create with the Magnificent Source.

We can experience the higher consciousness within each of the simple good feelings we experience from the acts and expressions of love, care, kindness and compassion. The ability and strength to forgive, forget and let go needs something more than what is within our body and mind's capacity. It comes from our being. We need to make a connection to our core being and to the higher consciousness in order to experience this higher consciousness.

How about the expressions and experiences of the graceful flow? A couple of times while presenting my Toastmaster speeches, I experienced this strange feeling. During every sentence I was speaking I felt I was lost at the end of the sentence. But just as I finished the sentence, words for the next sentence flowed to me. Not one time, but for almost every sentence until I was at least halfway through my eight-minute speech. It was beyond an amazing experience, to receive the flow of right words to me just in the moment I needed them. What is this called? Wasn't I driven by a higher consciousness?

When I am completely involved and loving what I am doing, whether presenting a speech, writing an interesting blog or doing yoga, I experience this graceful free flow of energy. It feels so ecstatic and blissful! Isn't it a spiritual experience?

Spiritual Transformation

Do you recall times like this? Probably you experience this unexplained flow many times in a day. When we are doing our passionate work or loving what we are doing with absolutely no resistance—we are living at our highest potential and are connected to our spiritual self!

Sometimes just being in the presence of someone seems to permeate feelings of love, joy and peace. Those people are radiating this divine spiritual energy. Love, light, joy, peace, kindness, compassion, forgiveness and gratitude are some of the high-level energies. Receiving these kinds of high energies from someone, or experiencing these high-energy vibrations within our own self, is a result of our connection to the Divine Spirit.

"When we have the Divine Spirit within us, why is it that we are not always filled up with these high energies?" The answer is, because we are given the freedom to choose to do what we want, and execute our will power the way we want. We have both ego and the Divine Spirit within us. Consciously or sub-consciously we slip and disconnect ourselves from our Divine Spirit. That is when we are operating by our ego.

That is when we get bogged down in negative energies, such as worry, fear, anxiety, guilt, sadness, hurt, living in blame or resentment. We don't need to feel bad about what happened or for getting involved in the negative energies. We just can get to the conscious thought that we don't need to be in the negative energies, and choose to get connected to the Divine Spirit and get into the higher energies of love, joy and peace.

By connecting to the Divine Spirit, we let go of our ego and see ourselves as part of the Magnificent Source. We let go of our need to compete, to be right or to win. Rather, we choose to embrace love and peace. Living gets seemingly easier as we co-create. We overcome struggles and challenges

BUTTERFLY

easily as we put the problems into the hands of the Magnificent Source to take care for us.

By breaking free from the shackles of our own self and seeing ourselves as part of the Magnificent Source, we will literally be expanding our horizons from the limited to the boundless infinity. We get to live life in breeze and bliss.

Our core being is love, joy and peace. Feeling good and having love, joy and peace within us and seeing these good feelings and high-energy vibrations within others is experiencing spirituality.

When we see, experience and realize this spirituality, we naturally and instantaneously see the sense of interconnectedness and belongingness. We see each encounter as a blessing. We look for the best in every situation and a gift in every problem. We enjoy the flow of life, bring out the best in ourselves and contribute to the world with our best. Let's come out of our cocoons and live an absolutely gorgeous life, the life we are meant to live and love.

Self-reflections:

1. At my core, I am love, joy and peace. Any moment I feel I am not operating from this core being, it means I am being operated by my ego. I have a choice to connect back to the Divine Spirit within me.
2. When I am hurt or sad, asking, "Why am I hurt? Or why am I sad? Is it going to do any good for me being in this state? What can I do to restore my loving and peaceful being?" helps. By consciously transcending my thoughts to better feeling thoughts, to higher vibrating thoughts of love, joy, peace, enthusiasm—I can soar.
3. When stuck with something I do not know how to handle, I can get connected to the Source, surrender my problem

and seek help. Then I can rest in peace with assurance that I will find ways to resolve it.
4. I can choose to live with absolutely no blame or resentment. They are brakes to my loving, peaceful being. I have the magnificent potential to be what I want. I can get in connection with the Magnificent Source. Source guidance comes to me in many ways. Keeping my mind open and free allows the flow of miracles my way.
5. Doing what I love to do allows the love within me to flow richly and keeps me in a blissful state.

How Does It Feel to Experience Spirituality?

The graceful flow of life, living fully in the present moment, being at ease, seeing good naturally in any situation are some of the expressions of living in a higher consciousness and experiencing spirituality.

As I write the story of my illness and recovery 12 years from the day of it happening, my reflections of those times made me see my past life more vividly and I was touched even more deeply. It's beyond amazing to think of Dad's actions and the way of his being then. As a child I didn't have the opportunity to comprehend what Daddy meant by his words: "I believe in my work. My work is my God! Doing one's work with earnest sincerity and honesty is nothing but Godliness."

As I reflect upon the events surrounding my journey back to health, I can clearly see and feel what he meant by his words in the way he served me. For sure, some enormous strength moved through him.

He used to wake up early, get ready, and all his focus was on attending to my needs. I rarely saw pain, hurt or worry on his face.

He did each and every little thing for me with such intense care, so filled with love and joy: the fervid, zealous expressions in serving me a home-cooked, warm nutritious meal; the gentle love in giving me a helping hand to rise up and walk; during my hospital visits, running for a wheelchair, putting me on it and pushing me with sheer joy; a courageous expression to give me unwavering strength, support and inspiration to cope with the pain; monitoring my anemia by squeezing my fingertips, keenly observing the color of my lips and the membranes of my eyes; the most guileless, innocent expressions in asking for my help to see his newborn grandbaby. All these thoughts touch me deep down.

He did immerse himself so fully and handled everything with fervid joy and zeal. He was so focused on my needs, and nothing distracted him or pulled him down. The courage and strength he carried was truly beyond ordinary.

I now believe that Daddy was moved by a higher consciousness. The words he used to say … "Your life will turn green and flourish just as these leafless trees begin to sprout as spring starts," or "You hit the bottom of the valley and can't go any further. Your blood counts just have to come up." These are not words he thought inside his mind or prepared to say to me. They just erupted through him in the moment. I now strongly believe that God (higher consciousness) acted through him, talked through him and moved through him during those times.

Each of my family members' love, care and concern was just as unique, and I just can't imagine my survival without any of them. In spite of all the stressful, challenging times we had, the biggest and the best things we, as a family, received were the deepening of our relationships, strength, support and reinforcement of positive faith! I feel beyond blessed to be showered with all the loving, caring, affectionate acts and thoughts, all the help and support I had from

Spiritual Transformation

my family, and the magnificent, diligent and compassionate works of my doctor.

I also believe Dr. Collins acted from a higher consciousness in my case. There was no protocol in my case because the cause of my condition was unknown. They finally gave my illness a name: idiopathic myelofibrosis. Idiopathic means "unknown cause"; myelo means "marrow"; and fibrosis means "scar." Strange as the name sounds, my unknown scar tissue started turning my life in a new direction and made me search for greater meaning.

Enjoy Being in the Stream

"I wonder why?" is so much better than "Why is it so?" Just say these two sentences out loud and see how it feels to you. "I wonder why she is upset!" "Why is she upset?"

How was your tone of voice? How were your emotions?

I bet your tone was softer on the first one where you expressed your wonder, while a question would have raised your tonal inflexion leaving you with an expectation.

Wonder leaves us in the mystery and zeal to know without attaching ourselves to the results. A child enters into this world just this way, with absolutely no desire, but full of zeal to explore the mystery.

As the child grows and starts experiencing things, she starts forming likes/dislikes, wants/hates, happiness/sadness, etc. Further, the child may start favoring some over others and prefer to stay in good feeling emotions. Instead of seeing the feelings coming from the inside, she mistakenly assumes that those feelings are generated from the external object, action or person and tries to hold on to that external connection. When those external objects disappear, her joy fades. Then she starts looking out and craving those external objects, which she imagined were the cause of her positive energies. Similarly, she misinterprets that the external object or person is the cause of her negative energies and starts pushing away those objects or people.

With the existing desires/hates, we get caught up in always wanting to experience the desires and fight against the unwanted ones. This endless loop of wanting to experience again and again what gave us joy, and resisting what we don't like, leaves us no time and desire to explore the new un-manifested world which is our true intrinsic nature. Thus we are distancing ourselves from our true intrinsic nature and the vigor and the zeal of a child. This process leads to putting on a tiring mask of repetitive patterns and having no desire to experience the unknown world.

The way to live a life full of joy and vigor is to enjoy the *doing* with no attachment to the results, and explore the un-manifested universe with pure joy.

When we surrender our acts, thoughts and experiences, we become without desire, with no anticipation, with no clogging of the mind. This creates an empty space in the mind for good things to flow to us.

Being open and enjoying the flow of experiences, without either clenching our fist for what we like or pushing away what we do not like—we can enjoy being in the stream of life's flow!

As Gita says, "Do the activities unattached to the results. Surrender your activities so your mind is free of both pleasure and pain; and be open to enjoy the present moment gracefully."

Live in the Present Moment

Deepak Chopra explained beautifully the idea called "The Present Moment" in his book *Power, Freedom and Grace*. To capture the visual picture of his explanation of "being here and now" I created the following image.

Spiritual Transformation

The Present Moment

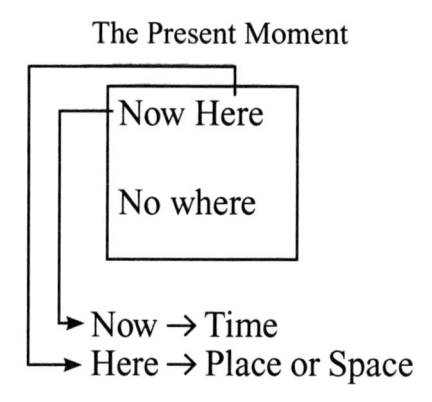

```
┌──────────────────┐
│ ┌──Now Here      │
│ │                │
│ │  No where      │
│ │                │
└─┼────────────────┘
  │
  └► Now → Time
  └► Here → Place or Space
```

What does it mean to live in "The Present Moment"? It means, being now, here and being nowhere else.

The words of my fellow Toastmaster Dewayne Wright during a table topic answer sticks with me. "Children live in the moment. All that they care for is the present moment. If you say we will play tomorrow or go to the museum next week, they don't care. All that they care about is what you do with them, *this moment*—the moment you have right now."

The only control we have control is over "The Present Moment." We can act, talk and think only in the present moment, not in the past or in the future. We can think of the past or future in this moment, but we can't act or talk in the past or the future. Do you see the difference? The only power we have of the past or future is to think, while in the present—we can think, act, and experience.

I wrote a poem to express my feelings.

> By living in the Present Moment fully,
> We will be just ourselves
> Enjoying ourselves
> Enjoying what we are doing

BUTTERFLY

We will be fully aware, focused, conscious
We let ourselves flow gracefully, with absolutely *no strings* attached.

By "no strings attached" I mean that we are not clinging to our past or resistant or obsessed about the future. We are just "here and now", enjoying it fully. We are at ease with ourselves, what is and whatever comes our way.

We frequently hear the expression, "Dance with your spirit." How does it make us feel when we hear this expression, or even just the word dance? We immediately relate it to fun, joy, ecstatic expressions or free spirits. Dance awakens the inner child-like spirit and brings it to life. We feel full of joy, blooming and blossoming.

It's an activity which makes us involved completely, with spontaneous free will and with literally no resistance. It's something that flows out of us naturally, like the gush of a tidal wave.

The word "dance" may not necessarily be the physical activity of dance, rather it could be any activity that emanates and expels our spirit to flow freely with literally no bounds. It could be playing a sport for an athlete; singing for a singer; painting for an artist. Whatever activities we are passionate about—the activity which makes us live fully, live in the moment and with joy and peace.

Yesterday I was watching an Indian movie titled "Chukkallo Chandrudu". In the movie, a girl named Shalini is a champion tennis player. Somehow she loses her focus; and after each inning she looks at the scoreboard. Her pulse races and her performance drastically plummets.

Then comes in the hero and boosts her by saying, "You are focusing on the results and winning, and that's why you are finding it hard. Quit looking at the scoreboard. Forget that it's a competition and a tennis match. Just watch the ball

Spiritual Transformation

that is coming, and dance with it. Enjoy the game, Shalini. Dance, Shalini, dance."

As we can guess, Shalini shifts her entire focus to the ball, beats the opponent in an incredible way and wins the game! It's only a movie, but it shows the results of immersing oneself completely and enjoying doing the activity with one's whole heart and soul. A miraculous change occurred in a mere couple of minutes. However, there is a great point that we all can tremendously benefit from implementing: *No matter what the results are, we feel fuller, more complete and happier when we are living in the moment.* Enjoy living fully in the "Present Moment," with no strings attached, with no expectations or resistance to anything.

The daily activities where we felt we were completely ourselves, transported to a heavenly world; where we weren't bothered about anything else in this world—that is living in the moment! This activity could be even just sitting quietly, calming the mind. Finding ways to incorporate more of such activities or spending even more time doing what we are already doing gives us an opportunity to live in the moment longer. Even if we don't find new activities, just being ourselves makes a difference—makes our spirit dance, and enjoy fully doing whatever we are doing. This makes our life and our spirit dance with joy!

When we liberate ourselves from all the attachments, conditions and limitations, we allow ourselves to glide through the stream of life as a free bird, with the experience of newness, richness and bliss in each moment of our life. By living in the "Present Moment," we learn to let go, be receptive to giving and receiving unconditionally and accept what is. We live free of worry, guilt, hurt and anxiety.

Worry, guilt and hurt are of the past while fear and anxiety are about the future. By bringing awareness to the "Present Moment," which is fresh and new, all the problems, worries, anxiety and pain will be dissolved. By practicing living in the moment, we learn to let go of many thoughts and become a silent observer of our thoughts.

For example, when we watch a movie of someone undergoing challenges, being the observer we feel their emotions. But we don't let those feelings or emotions affect us for long and can simply let them go. On the other hand, when we go through the same scenario that has a greater impact on us, we find it quite difficult to let go. But by practicing living in the present moment, we become an observer of our own thoughts, we learn to not judge and let go of those thoughts without letting them impact us much. We learn to remain unattached to both positive and negative emotions. It doesn't mean we are uncaring. Rather it allows us to live a life of freedom and grace.

Be "here and now." Fully enjoy ourselves and what we are doing each moment.

PERFORM ACTS, AND SURRENDER THEM!
Bhagavad Gita, chapter 3, verse 19, last line

asakto hyaacharankarma paramaapnoti puurushah

Translation: *By performing actions without attachment, one attains the Supreme.*

I wonder, why don't we maintain the same excitement and enthusiasm we have while pursuing goals after achieving them? Is it the inactivity, or is it the knowing, or is it boredom of repetition that diminishes the vigor in us?

After thinking about some activities, I realized that it is not the repetition that causes us to lose vigor. If it were true, we wouldn't be enjoying our daily sleep and daily shower, would we?

Spiritual Transformation

It is because we leave those activities out of our minds the moment we are done with them. We don't linger upon how sweet and nice our sleep and showers are. We don't cling to them, nor do we resist them. We simply enjoy them, and once done, they are forgotten. That is why they last forever, and they are always dear to us. Every time we have them, we experience them with a breath of freshness. Once done, they are forgotten. That is the key for us relishing them forever.

Let's look into some of the routine activities we enjoy every time we do them such as: enjoying breakfast; driving to work; being at work; doing yoga/meditation; writing; reading; conversing with people.

Of course, never can any two activities be just the same. Even if everything else is the same, the time when they are done is still different. With time, many attributes change. We are not the very same person we were the previous moment. We might be performing the task with a different mindset or a different set of conditions.

From the manifested or un-manifested point of view, we always experience the unknown thrill when we move to an un-manifested plane. When we forget our works or deeds or activities once they are done, it is like putting back the works into the un-manifested world, and we explore them again with a fresh mind.

Enjoy fully what we are doing, and then drop it.

Bhagavad Gita, chapter 2, verse 47, first line:
Karmanya eva adhikaraste ma phaleshu kadachana
Translation: *Our right is to work and never to their results*

The same can be said as "perform actions, and surrender them." It is the way to experience eternal bliss.

Butterfly

Each Encounter is a Blessing

Everyone we encounter in our life is a blessing. Some people are easy to love and connect with. Some are not so easy. And some even push our buttons. Yet, each person we have encountered is a gift and a blessing as each has helped us to discover certain parts of ourselves better. Each encounter has brought to our awareness what we like, what we resonate with, what makes us excited, what we would like to change, what we will not tolerate. No matter whether the experience is pleasant or unpleasant, each has been a learning experience, and we grew because of it.

Those who have children would have discovered how much each child has shaped our personality. We would also have seen and experienced how different each child is, and how uniquely each contributed in our own learning, tuning and morphing. For some of those who are not a parent, at least you may have heard from your parents or friends say this.

We learn in different ways: teaching, coaching, self-study and self-analysis or through feedback from others. It's either explicitly told or implicitly realized as our own reflections. Sometimes I am not even aware of who I am and how I am doing unless I hear honest constructive feedback. That simple feedback has helped me many times in correcting, fine-tuning and even in excelling myself. Though we have to make personal effort in bringing in change and growth in ourselves, with help, guidance, training, feedback, mentoring and coaching we can leverage our growth many more times. Being part of others expands our horizons to explore and experience some similarities, dissimilarities, some totally unique experiences and a multitude of feelings.

We discover not only our strengths and likings, but also our weaknesses, dislikes, intolerance, qualities we appreciate and qualities we look upon to change, learn from and build

SPIRITUAL TRANSFORMATION

upon. The experiences of connections and relationships with other people are rewarding and enriching and are also opportunities for us to see self-reflections. Others' responses are like mirrors of us. When we see others having fun with us, it makes us aware that we are a fun person to be around. When others feel loved and appreciated around us, it brings us satisfaction that we are a loving person people appreciate to be around. Others are giving an opportunity to make changes to our personalities, to live higher fulfilled and purposeful lives.

We experience the process of giving/receiving, inspiration, sharing, mutual growth and fulfillment only in our encounters with others. Having gratitude for each person we meet in our life puts us immediately into higher energies. No matter what, there is always at least one thing we can discover or have learned from that person. Focusing our attention on that quality and being thankful for the person who made it possible keeps us connected and automatically takes off our minds from what we don't like and what we don't want to attract.

We are here to experience love, light, joy and peace. People are sent to us to help us experience more richness and take our life to the next higher level. Let us see love in others and the wrapped blessing we are sent to experience. Let's be thankful for each encounter we make with another person.

I am so thankful to each of you for being the beautiful blessings in my life. Thank you, thank you, thank you!

Self-reflections:

1. Are there any limitations I set on myself? Do I consider I have to be a certain way, speak a certain way or get things done a certain way? If so, these are hindrances for me to be my open-free self. Let me release those brakes, and enjoy being my true self.

BUTTERFLY

2. Do I ever incur in thoughts of worry, guilty or hurt? During those times, bringing my attention to the reality helps—I am thinking of the past, and I cannot change the past—the past is gone. If there is a lesson from the past, I can take the lesson and move on. It helps to let go and move on. I can make the best of the present moment.
3. Enjoy fully what I am doing. Then surrender the act. This helps in freeing me from any expectations or disappointments.
4. I see each person I encounter as a blessing. I look for the good in every encounter and situation, even if the experience is not a pleasant one.
5. Letting go of any blame or resentment liberates me. A way to let go is to forgive and forget. It does more good to me than the person who hurt me. Letting go is needed to live a fuller life.
6. Do I let someone else's words or actions bother me? No one or no situation can bother me unless I give my permission. Bringing my attention to the good and joyful things I want helps in taking off my mind from what bothers me.

BE COMFORTABLE AND AT EASE WITH WHO YOU ARE

Accepting ourselves the way we are, being comfortable and at ease with who we are and letting go of whatever prevents us to be our fuller self is vital to living the life we are designed for—a life full of love, joy and peace.

BEING VULNERABLE

I am involved with many thoughts and ruminations on being vulnerable. What is vulnerability? Why is it important to me? How does it contribute in building and strengthening relationships—both with the self and with others?

Spiritual Transformation

To be honest, I didn't fully know the meaning of the word vulnerable until the past few months. It used to be one of those strange words that I seem to understand when I look up the meaning but forgot the very next time I encounter it.

When I ask myself if I have been vulnerable while I was ill or during my divorce, I'd have to say indeed I was. I didn't think about it then, nor did I know the meaning of the word back then.

I got to fully know the meaning after I presented my Toastmaster speech, "Become the Change You Desire!" In this speech I admitted some of the challenges I faced in my speaking and how I am overcoming some of them. My friend Prakash actually helped me to fully understand and appreciate what it means to be vulnerable.

He wrote to me: "You asked me a while ago about the meaning of the word 'vulnerable.' I was waiting for a right opportunity to respond and I think this is the time. You really don't need to know the definition of it, because you embody that word and you live it much more than most people. Many details you shared are proof that you have this incredible attribute. It's one thing to know the definition of something and a whole other state of existence to actually live it. Your most recent speech was about you being vulnerable in front of an audience and admitting to your obstacles. It was very impressive to see the courage you showed in talking about your shortcomings, like you weren't audible enough, your words weren't quite understandable to others, and the ways you admit your shortcomings and make efforts to overcome those challenges."

Since that speech, I seemed to attract more articles on the appreciation of this quality of being vulnerable and my pondering continued.

Many times we are unwilling to expose the unusual or not so good parts of us, with the fear of losing our identity, or fear of losing approval and acceptance of others, or just because we are not comfortable doing it.

Listening to the audio program of Craig Valentine, 1999 World Champion Toastmaster speaker, brought to my consciousness the importance of being vulnerable and cherishing my own courage in openly admitting my mistakes, pitfalls and my weak points. Indeed it is a quality needed to accept our own self the way we are. It is fully needed for one's personal growth to step up and ask for help, and to connect to other people at a deeper level.

Being vulnerable includes two attributes:

1. Fully accepting our self the way we are, with all the good, bad and ugly parts.
2. Being transparent to let others see through our masks by admitting and sharing.

By being authentic, and showing the audience one's pitfalls, the speaker is leveraging rapport with his or her audience.

Just before I started writing this book about the two major challenges of my life, as per my friend Ravindra's recommendation I read Lance Armstrong's book *It's Not About the Bike*. Although I knew of the controversies about Lance Armstrong, I still wanted to check out his book to see how his writing flowed. It was very easy for me to get into this book as I went through a very similar process of diagnosis, procedures and coming close to death. Armstrong was raised by a single mom and inspired by his own mom. I could relate to this portion as well and quickly got an idea of how to unfold my own story.

As I began to write the stories of my illness and my divorce, I felt as if I was going through all of it again; this time with even greater emotions and a deeper awareness. It gave me another opportunity to reflect, appreciate and convey my

Spiritual Transformation

gratitude to the many wonderful blessings I received and keep receiving. It wasn't easy writing at times.

There were times when I cried, times I wondered why should I dig through the past and go through all those emotions, and times when I got stuck, not wanting to write the complete details, especially the negative feelings. But finally I managed to share enough to give the information and keep the story moving. I choose to be vulnerable at places with a hope that my vulnerable details could help someone to relate or resonate with their own story.

Writing is indeed one of the beautiful ways to connect to ourselves fully. The best things can flow through us only when we are open and free.

Why do we get connected to one who is vulnerable? It is because we see that person as more real, human, just like us, and we all have some not-so-good qualities, errors and pitfalls too. Being vulnerable and revealing one's weaknesses, mistakes or failures lessens the barrier between the two parties. We become more at ease and connect better.

It takes courage and strength to be willing to be vulnerable. But once we open up, it offers a road map for a happy, joyful, confident and exciting transformation.

Say How You Feel

Many times we are at ease and comfortable in sharing something exciting, but not the bad events in our lives. We hesitate before asking for help. If it is not something we can share at ease with everyone, we stumble even more. We might even think, *Should I ask this? Will it be of any help to the other person? Will I bother the other person by dumping my stuff? What would the other person think of me when I share?* Or it may not be any of these. It's just that we are not clear ourselves of the thoughts going on in our minds and don't know where to start or what to ask.

BUTTERFLY

But asking someone for guidance, or making a phone call and talking to someone when our mind is unclear and crazy helps. Just talking to simply vent out helps as well.

With the right person, we will feel so peaceful after the call. By speaking our thoughts out loud, we clarify our thoughts. The words of the other person or questions of the other person trying to understand what we are conveying will simply help us discover more of ourselves when we pour out our unclear thoughts.

Even if we hesitate and stumble, later when we look back, we realize that our relationships got stronger and deeper by sharing not just the common ordinary things, but by revealing the inner self which includes our mistakes, guilt, fluttering, stuttering and disorganization; the self that is struggling for clarity, which others don't normally see.

It not only helps the person who is sharing, but also helps the person who is listening to us. We are giving them an opportunity to see the deeper side of us, as well as for the other person to go deeper into themselves; so deeper touching and deeper connectivity happens.

We all need a few close ones, whether friends, family or colleagues; those with whom we can share not just the good or the comfortable parts of us, but also the difficult, unclear and ugly parts of ourselves.

The next time we hesitate to share, we can remember to step ahead and share or ask for guidance with no hesitation. We could be helping not only ourselves, but also the other person. Thus we could be mutually growing, learning and transcending. A relationship is more fulfilling when we are involved in the process of giving and receiving. And giving and receiving both occur simultaneously in the process of sharing our deeper self. It would uplift the hearts of others as we are opening us to them with a trust and honor in them. I am blessed to have a family and a few good friends with whom I can be fully

SPIRITUAL TRANSFORMATION

vulnerable without the fear of rejection or disapproval of me. Yes, it is not an easy thing to get there. But it has to start somewhere if we truly care for our personal growth. We would need to liberate ourselves from any negative energies of guilt, low self-esteem and fear. In this process we will strengthen our relationship with ourselves as well as with others.

Let's have the courage to be ourselves and say how we feel.

WHOLE IS BETTER THAN JUST GOOD

Whole is a lot better than just good. We can live fully and splendidly only when we accept and embrace not just the good and perfect parts of ourselves, but also what we thought as the not-so-good parts, which we usually suppress and bury within us.

Is this true?

Do we accept and embrace our mistakes? Are we perfect beings who have never made mistakes? Of course, our answer is "no." Let's be glad that we are not an alien to the human world. "To err is human!" Why is it important to accept and embrace ourselves wholly? Let's look at some of the common negative energies we humans experience: worry, anxiety, fear, guilt and frustration.

What impact do they have on us? They take away our peace and act as blocks to experience our fuller selves. We do not deserve to have this friction, this resistance—like brakes keeping us away from a part of us. Only when we learn to accept and embrace everything in us, we can enjoy the total freedom to live a fuller and richer life. When we are suppressing or burying something within us, it becomes a blockage to experiencing our fuller selves.

These blockages can be either thoughts we suppressed to gain approval and acceptance of our loved ones or to maintain a public persona; or the exciting thoughts we had in the moment to become something, but later suppressed them thinking we are not worthy enough or talented enough to become it.

When we haven't learned to accept and embrace certain unpleasant thoughts, such as "selfishness is bad," we are probably holding on to something we all are taught as kids.

But is selfishness really bad? Is taking care of us bad? Is being responsible for our own life bad? If we are not happy and don't love ourselves, how can we love someone else? Can we truly give out happiness when we are not happy within?

I see many moms working so hard to take care of their children, spouses and everything at home. But they don't take time to take care of themselves. But can we truly give our best when we are not taking good care of ourselves? My friend Radhi keeps reminding me that on a flight, we are told to put on our own oxygen mask first and then our child's. We have to take good care of ourselves first in order to give good care to our dependents.

Selfishness is holding what we have to ourselves. Instead of telling children "selfishness is bad," how about giving focus to *what we want* to teach them? Can we reframe our words to encourage our children to share what they have, co-create and have fun in sharing and giving?

When we accept and embrace our *whole* self—both the good and bad parts of ourselves—we liberate ourselves and truly enjoy the freedom of being ourselves. It is not the freedom our friends give. It's not the freedom and rights we are given at our work place. It is not the freedom we are given at home by our family members. I don't mean the freedom we are giving ourselves from the outside, but the freedom we give to within us, the self-acceptance.

If we have no limitations whatsoever, what kind of person do we want to be? Are we that now? If yes, great! We are on the most joyful path we deserve. If not, let's take courage to break those shackles that we are holding to. Are there any

SPIRITUAL TRANSFORMATION

suppressing thoughts we have in an attempt to maintain our public persona. Let's bring to light the limitations we placed on ourselves, thoughts that say we can't be this or that. Dig through any unveiled thoughts that are hindering us from being our higher self. Think of any negative thoughts we are holding or experience when we encounter a person or a situation.

We have every possibility to become what we want and fulfill every dream we thought of. We have every opportunity to dissolve and let go of the negative energies that are preventing us from enjoying our fuller selves.

And all the potential we need is just within us. It is in our loving, peaceful selves. It becomes part of us when we accept and embrace everything as is. Then nothing can break us or tear us apart. We can be the shiny, sparkling person we want to be. We can live a life in bliss, peace and grace!

Consider the negative thought, "I can't stand it." We mistakenly think the thought is caused by the people, circumstances or events around us. The truth is, we are feeling charged not because of what happened on the outside, but rather because of what is on our inside.

Let me illustrate what I mean. It was a pretty normal morning. My son and I were getting ready to get to his school and my work. My son screamed, "Mommy, Mommy, my milk got spilled on the carpet." What follows?

The devil inside me came out. "You spilled again? How many times have I told you, but you never get it? Already we are running behind." I fuss and fume and clean up the mess and am upset. Poor boy. He is infused with all my negative upset feelings too.

As I was reading *The Shadow Effect* by Debbie Ford, I realized that. It was not the external event of my son messing the carpet that triggered my negative energies. Rather it was my un-acceptance of my carpet getting messed up that was the main cause of my charge—my negative energy.

BUTTERFLY

I never learned to accept and embrace the fact that it is okay to accidentally spill something. I used to be unhappy even when I did it myself.

When I brought that acceptance within myself, I began to handle this kind of scenario much better. Now both my son and I are letting go and reconnecting back to our good feelings more quickly. So our responses and reactions are not the effects of what is happening on the outside, but are the results of what is *inside* of us.

Note that accepting and embracing something doesn't mean we have to like it or appreciate it or do it often; it just means we accept its presence. When we judge, we find it disturbs the peace within us.

When we embrace what is inside of us *fully* and *wholly* instead of just the good parts of us, we enjoy the total freedom of being ourselves, and we bring out the best in us. It is so draining to hide, mask, suppress and hold on to anything that disturbs our peace and prevents us from being our true selves. It is a lot easier and more graceful to live with absolutely no resistance and maintain a poised state. When we live fully, freely and openly, we transform and transcend; and we make a positive impact and a positive difference in other people's lives as well!

Who Are We?
>Are we our name?
>Are we our profession?
>Are we our qualities?
>Are we the roles we hold?

Each of these may identify us in some ways, but nothing can fully define who we are.

>I write out the following to revel in my affirmations:
>I am Beautiful

Spiritual Transformation

I am Loving
I am a Clear, Open Communicator

While these are some of my strengths and goals, I don't always project these aspects of myself. I can recall times where I exhibited less than ideal qualities. Thinking of my thoughts later used to create guilt or stress, and I'd give an explanation of why I was so.

Now I realize that none of those afterthoughts were needed. I am what I am in the moment, and it is just fine for that moment. It shows the truth of the statement, "Don't define yourself. Life becomes stale".

In the Bhagavad Gita, chapter 3, verse 30, the Super-Soul Krishna tells Arjuna, *"Therefore, O Arjuna, surrendering all your works unto Me, with mind intent on Me, and without desire for gain and free from egoism and lethargy, fight."*

I think the works mentioned can be physical activities, any past history, any thoughts of past or future—either positive or negative. When we define ourselves as being honest, friendly and compassionate, and we don't project these qualities, we tend to beat ourselves up and waste the current moment. Giving up our personal history is liberating and lets us be our deserved higher, spontaneous, free selves.

After a conversation, I sometimes think, *Oh, maybe I didn't convey my thoughts well in the way I intended. And this is not the only time. I do this way too many times; I am not a very spontaneous person. I am a tubelight.*

I now replace those thoughts with these words: *Whatever I do, think, say or ask for, I do with ease, comfortably and confidently.* Period.

No matter how I did, or what I said, I express my mind. Period. No regrets. No apologies. No thinking if I hurt him. No guessing if I could have said it clearer, nicer or sweeter to her.

Butterfly

This simple practice has been so liberating for me. Now I feel that making peace with myself and keeping my mind clear and free is much more important than being nice, good or sweet.

Recently I went through a short phase where I felt anxious and even felt a bit disconnected with myself. I spilled how I was feeling in that moment in an email to my siblings. As I was about to click on the send button, I thought for a second, *I might be just fine tomorrow or even in a couple of hours. Why should I unnecessarily make my siblings anxious too?* My next thought was, *It is okay to convey my current thoughts and feelings. When they change, I can convey the changed ones too. It gives me support and strength and I will connect to myself when I share what is on my mind rather than keeping to myself.* So I sent the email.

As I expected, it raised the concerns in my siblings and they contacted me. But by that time, I had spoken to my dear friend Radhi who helped me to spiral up again. My brother was happy I had shared my feelings. He said, "That is okay to talk and is even better for us to know how you are feeling especially in a not so good state, rather than not knowing anything."

"That's true! And now I am sharing those better feelings." Of course, it is not my intent to raise concerns or anxiety in my dear ones. What is more important for me is to spiral up and do whatever it takes to be connected to myself.

The point I am trying to convey here is that feelings are fleeting. We go through many emotions. We might project varied qualities and aspects in us in different moments. It is completely healthy to accept and show our vulnerable self. All this is possible when we don't rigidly define ourselves. Rather, accepting ourselves the way we are, accepting our varied forms, allowing the self to be at ease with whoever

SPIRITUAL TRANSFORMATION

we are and whatever we are projecting in any given moment. This is the key for living a stress-free life.

We don't need to define who we are. Instead we can allow ourselves to gracefully accept all different forms we might take.

Be sweet, be blessed!

Self-reflections:

1. Am I willing to accept all qualities within me? There is really nothing good or bad. What is important is to be at peace with who I am. Accept and embrace myself fully, just the way I am. This is the first step in letting go and to be my free, peaceful self.
2. Am I afraid to ask for help thinking others might think less of me? By asking, I am taking courage to learn, get better and stay stronger. I don't need to be afraid to ask because of our fear of rejection. By asking, I am taking fair chances to get my needs and wants met. There is nothing to lose. Many people want to help me.
3. Am I comfortable being myself in every situation? Or do I repent, regret, brood, or re-play tapes like, "I shouldn't have said that," "I shouldn't have asked," "I should have been nicer."? If so, be at peace knowing I did the best possible I could do in the given time, with the given circumstances. It's done. I can let it go, and bring attention to the present moment.
4. Do I rigidly define myself? If so, I can give up my definition of who I am. I can allow myself to gracefully experience all different forms of me.
5. Do I hesitate to be vulnerable? It takes much strength to be vulnerable and being vulnerable enhances the relationships with people to whom I confess.

BUTTERFLY

THE HIGHEST FORM OF ENERGY

What is the highest form of energy? Without a second's thought, it is love. Love is so powerful. Love is blind. True love is unconditional. We need no reasons to love. At the core, we are loving beings. We are full of love, born to experience love and share love.

OUR CORE BEING

My sister-in-law forwarded me a beautiful message by Sri Sri Ravi Shankar on perfection. The main points of the message are:

"Deep inside you are pure, you are innocent, you are beautiful. You are a most adorable person, most lovable person. Any imperfections are either your projections or perceptions of others."

This reminds me of the words, "If you ever find fault, find fault with the action or behavior, not with the person." Many parents try to implement this philosophy with their children. It is best to say the deed is wrong or is an unacceptable behavior. Yet we reinforce that we always love our children.

Though we believe in the message, we tend to forget it and say words like, "She is so rude," "He is so angry," "That is so stupid of her." The truth is, no one is a rude or an angry or a stupid person. It might just mean that he or she is unhappy or upset about something at that particular instant.

The next time we encounter this kind of self-talk, we can remember the above words, that each of us is pure love; we are beautiful at the core of our hearts. We are now seeing the other person's temporary projection or our temporary perception. By realigning to our true nature, the projections and perceptions automatically drop off.

Similarly, when someone catches us when we are in a bad mood, instead of getting burned with hurt, we can

Spiritual Transformation

consciously recall that we were simply projecting that undesirable quality at that particular time. Or perhaps the other person simply perceived us in an awful way at that particular moment because of their mindset in that particular moment. Projections and perceptions are fleeting and not the core of the person. What is core and true all the time is our pure, loving being. Love, light, joy and peace prevail!

I love this shanti mantra from Hindu Upanishads:

> *Om Asato Maa Sad Gamaya*
> *Tamaso Maa Jyotir Gamaya*
> *Mrityor Maa Amritam Gamaya*
> *Om Shanti Shanti Shanti*
> Translation: *The Supreme Universe! Please lead me from untruth to truth, from darkness to light, from death to immortality. Peace, peace, peace.*

In reality, there are no dualities. It is just absence of one leading to the other. When we bring light to a dark room, darkness simply disappears. By bringing truth, untruth vanishes. Similarly, there is no bad, evil or hatred. It is simply a lack of love. When love shines, bad, evil and hatred disappear. When joy shines, sadness disappears. When peace shines, agony disappears.

Let go of the fleeting projections and perceptions and stay connected to our core. As the poem tells us, "We are pure love, the most adorable person, and the most lovable person!"

Love Yourself!

We should love ourselves. Why is it so important?

We are naturally born loving beings! We are made of love. We feel good when we feel loved and love ourselves. When we love ourselves, we are connected to our source

BUTTERFLY

creation, the Divine Spirit, and are feeling at our best. We are filled with positive energies. The moment we digress into negative energies, we disconnect from our source creation. We don't feel good and don't feel loved. When we don't feel loved, we cannot give out love; as we can't give what we don't have.

To test this we can ask within us, "How am I feeling now?" Our answers could vary anywhere from: "great," "exceptional," "terrific," "good," "loving," "enthusiastic," "joyous," "okay," "not bad," "not so good." We can use this question as a barometer of our feelings.

Next, if your answer is "good" or any of the other positive feelings, great. If not, we can make a shift to focus on things we love, those activities that move our heart. The more we feel loved, the more we are able to love. What we are on the inside shows through and spreads outwardly. When we come in contact with others either in person or in thoughts, we radiate outwardly these positive energies of love, joy and enthusiasm.

By doing this, we are bouncing back to our natural loving state. We are love and are filled with love. We need to stay in touch and connect to our loving being, and if we ever digress, we need to make a shift to come back on track.

Every morning in our home, we have the same routine. My son resists waking up, brushing his teeth, eating his cereal. He cries and complains, and I yell at him: "You have to do these things and we need to leave on time." It is not the best way for both of us to begin the day—filled with negative energies.

And then I chose to change this. I still tell him what he has to do and then I step aside and utter the affirmation I obtained from Rhonda Byrne's book *The Power:* "I am feeling good. I feel good. I am amplifying my good feelings. Life is responding to my good feelings." As if magic happens

Spiritual Transformation

in front of my eyes, I see him slowly moving, walking to me to give me a hug, and then following the sequential steps to get ready for the day. The result is that we both are filled with good, positive energies. We start taking care of what we have to in a pleasant, nice way and we get connected back to our natural loving selves.

Deepak Chopra once said that you should not try to clench the water of the flowing stream in your fist. Instead, put your palm in the stream of water and enjoy the flow of water. He was saying to be our natural loving selves—to stay connected by allowing us to follow the natural flow of giving and receiving. Let us enjoy the stream of our life journey.

Love is Blind

"Love is blind" is a popular expression we hear. What does it mean?

Love is beyond sensory perceptions. Love doesn't need reasoning or intellect. Love is a blissful state of being that naturally flows. We are created out of love. We are natural loving beings. The moment we start attaching conditions and expectations to love, it evaporates. Pure love is unconditional.

One day when I shared my thoughts of practicing unconditional love, one of my cousins posed an interesting question. "Most of the people these days are interested only in needs-based relationships. Once their needs are fulfilled, they don't even smile at you; if they come across you, they don't have a sense of gratitude. Do these people deserve unconditional love?"

This is not an uncommon question, for someone in their 20s. I would have probably felt the same had someone asked me to practice unconditional love a few years back. There are times I remember when my dad said, "Just give, give, give, give with a pleasant smile, whatever you are asked for, whatever you do."

BUTTERFLY

I burst out, "I can't be that person, I am just not that person."

My thoughts have changed now. Of course, still I am not a 100 percent unconditional loving person, but I totally believe in being unconditionally loving, unconditionally giving. It's the way I maintain my natural loving and peaceful being. It's not to please someone, or make someone else happy, but more importantly, I hold these values of being in love and peace within myself.

Now to answer my cousin's genuine question about whether people who don't reciprocate kindness or good will and don't have gratitude deserve unconditional love? I feel that in spite of whether they deserve love or not, it helps *us* to love them, rather than not to love. When we do not love, we are not being our natural self. Just think of when you are angry with someone—you cease to be your natural self. It takes a lot more energy to be unnatural than to be your peaceful self. Doesn't it?

Few relationships or deeds are reciprocating in the same way.

Think of the most common relationship between parents and children. Parents love their children unconditionally. As infants and toddlers, most of the giving is from the parents' side, and the receiving from the children. Still, parents take joy in giving fully and cherish it. They feel good to be able to take care of their children and give them the best. That is unconditional love. They take care of their children with no expectations.

We never get to reciprocate the same way for our parents, the way they took care of us. But, what we are called upon to do is take care of our children in a similar way our parents took care of us.

It's much easier to love someone rather than hate or be angry with someone. We might not realize it, but this is the

Spiritual Transformation

truth. It takes so much of our negative energies to not be loving and happy—with whatever we encounter.

Of course it might not be easy to love unloving people, uncaring people, negative people or those who hurt us. But definitely it is much easier on us to let go of the negative feelings and be our free natural self.

We can't call ourselves loving when we have restrictions on love. If we love only loving people, or people whom we care about, and not the rest, how can we be fully loving? We have all experienced forgiveness or have been treated outstandingly from someone unknown.

It always has to start with someone. One has to give for the other to receive.

It's not always possible to reciprocate immediately, or ever. No one is required to be reciprocal. I think what we are called upon is to be who we are from our heart, close to our true, pure, natural and peaceful self. Just be the person you want to be and are happy to be. Go by your inner guidance of what makes you be your loving, peaceful self.

Pure love is blind. It needs no reasons to love and to be loved. Love is unconditional.

Self-reflections:

1. When I am hurt by someone's actions, do I find fault with the person or with that particular act? Let me restrict the hurt to the act, not to the person. We all are loving beings at the core. No one wants to hurt anyone deliberately.
2. How am I feeling? Good, great, love, peace? If so, great! If not, let me consciously get connected to the core being, and become the love and peace I want to be.
3. Say out loud, *I am feeling good. I am amplifying my good feelings.* See how it feels.

BUTTERFLY

4. Do I have feelings of anger, hatred or resentment towards anyone? If so, I am pulling away from my core being by holding on to the venom that is destroying me. The easiest way to liberate me is to send out love to all the negative energy I am holding. Love dissolves all the negative energies and liberates me to enjoy my free and fuller self.
5. Be the love and peace I meant to live and enjoy.

Part 4:

Raising My Son

Part 4
Raising My Son

Raising a child as a single mom is not easy, and it could be challenging at times. The good news is—the single mom could become a person with more strength and courage. We learn to embrace and find much joy in many of the simple everyday gestures. You could be under more financial pressures in taking care of all the living expenses by yourself for you and your children because you are obligated to work, with few fallback options.

Besides financial pressures, single moms are challenged with the physical demands and also the emotional security of the family. Again, the payoff for all this is gaining more strength, courage and learning to seek more ways to get our needs met. On a positive note, we will have the freedom to make our life and our children's lives the way we want them to be. We become 100 percent responsible for our life and our children's lives, which brings more satisfaction and gratification.

To me, in some ways it was even more challenging, living thousands of miles across the ocean from my immediate family. Fortunately, I never experienced any major struggles in raising my son. We take many things we have for granted. But when we miss something or someone important, it creates a big vacuum. The situation may not even be painful, but I feel the lack of emotional security that comes when family is living close to me to lean on or seek help from when needed.

BUTTERFLY

Fortunately, I had the opportunity to watch the birth of my nieces, Mona and Sindhu, and my nephew Pranav and watch them grow from babies to children. Those experiences certainly have helped me to raise my son, Keshav. Anna's family being in the U.S. and relatively at a closer distance of about 350 miles was of immense help and provided many opportunities to watch their children. Especially after my divorce they used to visit often and were a big help and a joy to be with. They were there for Keshav's first Christmas and first birthday and visited whenever they could until they left the States in March 2010 to be home with our parents.

Since Anna and Vadina lived in the U.S. for so long, I still check with them on any advice or suggestions I need for Keshav when he is sick, or with school questions, or just about anything. My parents being here in the U.S. several times and having watched kids grow can relate very well to my day-to-day life with my son. That ease to relate within the close family is one of the wonderful blessings I am grateful for. It indirectly offers so much strength and support.

My 4-year-old son still sleeps in my niece Sindhu's crib. After Sindhu, Pranav used it for a little while and they saved it so well and brought it all the way to my place and fixed it for my soon-to-be-born baby. Many of the cool clothing Keshav wears today belonged to his cousin Pranav's. Kudos to my Vadina for saving them so well and for so long and passing them on to me. It tickles me to recall Pranav wearing the shirts Keshav is wearing now. Once again, this sharing brings the warmth of the family close to us.

During my most stressful time, Amma came all the way from India to help me out and stayed for three months. My parents' age and health conditions aren't well-suited for these long journeys. Yet she made it, and it was of immense strength, help and support to me to take care of the many important things I had to handle at that time. The two major ones were filing for my U.S. citizenship and completing the paperwork for our divorce. Keshav was about 15 months old, and Amma kept him home and fully pampered him.

Staying miles across in a different country is what made us miss each other the most. Also, my parents felt helpless not being able to be with me, and I missed the opportunities to reach out to them. Yet there remains a bond wherever we are.

I have enormous regard and gratitude to the wonderful ladies Neelima and Uma who took care of my son until Keshav was two-and-a-half years old. I preferred the homecare instead of leaving him at a daycare while he was very small. It was such a comfortable feeling to leave my son with them in the morning, knowing that he was in good hands—to leave with no worry. I can't recall a day when tears stirred in my eyes to leave him or when I had those missed feelings. I enjoyed him when he was with me, and yet I was in comfort and peace when I had to leave him to go to work. I give my sincere thankfulness to the warm love and tender care they showered on my son. They not only took care of my son, but also helped me to start my day bright by exchanging a cheerful smile.

I am also thankful to the many local friends and families, who had extended their helping hands whenever I needed, or simply to cheer and lift us up. Once again, in the midst of the juggling, stressful times it is such a comforting feeling and strength that there are people around me who can help me during unforeseen times.

I can't say how blessed I am to have Judith, my colleague, to run to with any sort of help, guidance and suggestions I need with no inhibitions, and she patiently answers and offers guidance to many of my naive questions too. Besides her, her whole family is involved in giving Keshav a sense of belonging. It was wonderful of Judith to send her husband to

BUTTERFLY

have lunch with Keshav for the Father's Day luncheon they had at school. Since then, Mr. Sanders stops by now and then for a surprise visit with Keshav.

Love is in the air. People are sent my way to help me and shower both Keshav and me with many blessings. When Keshav stuck his fingers in the elevator and I was panicked, Ms. Jade from his aftercare simply walked with me and stayed with me in hospital emergency ward until we made sure it wasn't critical.

Now I don't feel very anxious about the future, because I keep seeing and experiencing all the abundance of help gracefully flowing my way. I am being left with poignant memories of all the wonderful people in our way every time I face some challenge. Good things keep flowing in unexpected ways, miraculously.

I feel blessed in ways to have people around me, whether friends, colleagues or Toastmasters, who are ready to willingly offer any sort of help I need. It is such a peaceful feeling to have this kind of extended support. Of course, my close ones are still a phone call away.

I can totally understand a single mom's overwhelming feelings with the thought of her or her children falling sick. What if I have to run to the doctor in the middle of the night, or have to run to the pharmacy? Can I handle it? It is especially stressful when the children are small, even to leave them alone to take a shower demands more planning, caution and alertness and can hike up the anxiety. Unless one is financially sound and can afford childcare beyond the working hours, one has to compromise on personal time, like having a gym workout, running a quick errand by oneself or shopping for oneself.

But children grow up fast, and both they and we outgrow many of these things. A child's cherubic nature and resilience pervades, and we quickly become like them, able to bounce back quickly and live in the moment. They become our soul mates and companions too—to laugh with, cry with, have fun with and even to argue with. With their everyday growth, our world expands as well, having to learn new things, finding new avenues to meet the needs.

Lessons from a 14-Month-Old Baby

I ran across my old journals, and the following comes from what I had written in September 2009:

Wouldn't it be a joyful life if we just needed to do what we love to do? Stop for a second and visualize the face of a happy baby. Look at that beaming, radiating smile. Hear the giggles. Why is this baby so joyful? Because he does what he wants to do, or maybe he just enjoys whatever he does. It doesn't matter whether they do what they love, or enjoy what they do. The crux is, the baby enjoys the present moment to the fullest, lives in a joyous way and permeates joy around them.

I have a 14-month-old baby boy. He is the joy of my life. I cherish each moment I spend with him. Watching him grow taught me some wonderful lessons. I would like to share three salient lessons I learned from him.

Lesson One: Explore Your Favorite Things

One day I called up my Anna and shared with excitement that I nicknamed my son as "Keshav Explorer."

"Keshav Explorer?" The way my brother stressed the word "explorer" conveyed confusion about why I chose that name.

I chuckled inside and said, "Yeah, Explorer! We use Internet Explorer to search for our favorite things on the Internet, and Windows Explorer to retrieve our files on our computers. Similarly, Keshav goes around hunting for some cool looking, tiny, comfy to touch articles, which he can easily carry and chew on as a lollipop. He even finds the items

BUTTERFLY

I haven't seen for a while—my favorite pen, the DVD remote, my special two-sided yellow-pink marker. He thoroughly enjoys each item he finds and he plays with it, glides his fingers all over to feel it, licks it, and even chews it if I don't catch him in time. That's why I named him Keshav Explorer!"

Anna and I burst out in laughter. Anna teased me that I am getting more creative with my baby. Maybe I am exploring myself.

LESSON TWO: BE LIGHTHEARTED

There are moments when I scold Keshav when he splashes his food or blows bubbles from the water he sips. Within a few seconds he is walking towards me with his arms outstretched beckoning me to hold him.

How many times do I take him away when he pulls the TV cable wires, and he goes back and tries to do it again? I get frustrated and upset. However, he remains poised, as if nothing happened. His cool, calm behavior makes me wonder how he is happy even when I am yelling at him. Maybe that's just the baby's way. They don't carry over hurt, pain or sadness. They leave their baggage of unpleasant things and move on with bubbly, enthusiastic spirits, with a cherubic face as if nothing can hurt them. He is teaching me a lesson—the lesson of not getting upset even though I am not enjoying the experience. I could be equally joyful if I practiced what he is doing: Don't carry hurts. Forgive, forget, and move on with a happy, smiley face. Be lighthearted.

LESSON THREE—SET NO LIMITS

We often hear, "I gave up learning swimming," or "I don't have the skills or talents to be a salesperson," and many more excuses? Have we seen a baby who gave up learning to walk? Or who hasn't flipped onto his tummy? Why so? It's because babies know no limits. They don't know that they cannot do it. And so they do it. They always keep reaching for above and beyond. I saw Keshav falling down many times. It doesn't stop him. He gets up and gets going. Watching him, I realized that the only limits we have are what we set ourselves.

These are some of the wonderful lessons I learned from my 14-month-old baby. I could be equally joyful as him, if I practice what he is doing: enjoy my favorite things; don't carry my hurts; forgive, forget, and move on with a happy, smiley face; be lighthearted; set no limits. I can literally achieve anything I want! It's up to me the way I want to be, and what I want to become.

Thank you, my little one. You have taught me some of life's beautiful lessons.

JUST RIGHT FOR ME

I wrote this in my journal in December of 2011:

I am thankful to my friend Radhi, who is the key person for me to get into these thoughts!

While I was asking for suggestions of what would be appropriate words to answer to my 3-year-old son's questions, she suggested that it is time for me to introduce him to the idea of different types of families.

She mentioned the lyrics of the Barney song, which she loves. My son and I watched Barney, and we loved it! Radhi even wrote out the lyrics of that song, which fit us:

A family is people and
A family is love,
That's a family.
They come in all different sizes
and different kinds,
But mine is just right for me,
Yeah, mine is right for me.

BUTTERFLY

After watching it, I was able to assertively say to my son that families come in different sizes and different kinds. Some have a mom, dad, brother, sister; some are larger families including grandma, grandpa; some are small with just mom and child, dad and child or grandma and child. Some include a stepbrother or a stepsister.

There is nothing good or bad about any of these families. They are just different families. Ours is small and just right for us, right now.

On the same subject, my friend Prakash suggested, "You also might want to talk to him about the fact that some children only live with one of the parents and perhaps point out those kids or families. You might also want to say that we are just a different kind of family, and do not use the words good or bad. Think of the two or three points you want to emphasize to him and repeat those points as often as you can, in different words, so he is at ease with your family. The key thing is you don't want him to feel uncomfortable about this subject as he grows older."

Before this, I wasn't fully prepared for what to tell my son, though it was always at the back of my mind—I avoided these thoughts. Now I realized that it is high time to be realistic and teach what is, rather than finding a temporary patch to tell in that moment and get by.

Hearing Radhi and Prakash's words, feedback from my siblings, thoughts from my own research and putting out all dormant thoughts in my own mind, I came up with the following conclusive thoughts:

First I need to let go of the uncomfortable feelings myself and just be comfortable with what is, the reality. Then I can teach my son better and can be a model to him. Kids learn and perceive mostly from our being, and beliefs, rather than mere words. It is even better if our talks are matching our way of living and our beliefs.

RAISING MY SON

I definitely want to teach and create a good sense of all the different family relationships: dad-mom; dad-son; mom-son; grandpa/grandma-grandson, uncle/aunt-nephew; as well as nieces, brothers, sisters and friends.

Just because I am not in a marriage doesn't mean I have a negative opinion of a traditional family or marriage or a couple. It was just that his dad and I couldn't continue together in a healthy way. Similarly, just because my son's dad is not in our lives right now, my son doesn't need to develop a negative opinion about a dad or the relationship between dad and child. Both of us just need to be comfortable with the subject of dad, mom and mom-dad.

Now I got into the comfortable spirits of talking openly about dad, whether my dad or some other child's dad, without having to be afraid if I am unnecessarily creating hurt feelings. I am now focused more on teaching and creating a comfortable and healthy learning experience for my son of all nurturing family relationships.

Anna's suggestion helped me when Keshav said, "I want my daddy. Where is my daddy? I want my daddy to come to me."

"I would persuade him to elaborate by asking what he means. What would he want to do with Daddy that he is not able to do? Get to the essence of what he means and what he is missing."

The next morning when Keshav said, "I want my daddy", I asked, "What would you like to do with your daddy?"

"I want to watch Barney with Daddy."

"Can I watch it with you?"

He answered, "Yes."

Later, I said, "Daddy could not be with us now. He loves you. For now I can be both Daddy and Mommy for you. Daddy loves you. Mommy loves you too."

BUTTERFLY

He seemed to be happy with what I said. Later that evening, when we were driving to the bookstore, he said, "Mommy, I want my daddy."

"What would you like to do with Daddy?"

"I want him to be here in the car with us."

I repeated what I said in the morning: "Daddy cannot be with us now. He is in a different place. Sometimes Mommy and Daddy cannot live together. Right now it is just Mommy and you. We are just a small family, and a different family. For now anything you want to do with Dad, I will do for you."

He seemed to be okay with my explanation.

I realize and empathize with my son wanting to spend time playing and sharing with his dad. But both my son and I need to accept what is, the reality that we don't have his dad in our lives now and just enjoy the way we are; the family with mom and child. We don't need to feel bad or miss something that we do not have. That is what I am intending to inculcate in him. I am willing to do my possible best by being both dad and mom for him to the extent permissible to me.

At the same time, I want to leave the channel open and with positive hopes and good feelings of the "dad figure" and the relationship of dad-son, and all other possible nurturing relationships.

In a nutshell, I would like for him to be comfortable to be the way we are, without the feeling that he is missing out; yet with positive hope and good feelings for the possibility of a new family configuration.

Everything is just right for me. The experiences I had in the past and the situations I am in are just right for me. I do truly believe Dr. Wayne Dyer's words: "There are no accidents in this universe. Everything happens for a reason." All the experiences I've had were needed to provide me with the energy to propel me to a higher spiritual frequency. If I am better than I used to be that is a good reason to make peace with myself. Everything is just right for me!

Whatever I was, I was just right with the values, knowledge and experiences I had at that particular time. Whatever I am, I am just right, with my current values, knowledge and the experiences I have up to this point.

Abraham Hicks tells us to tell a better-feeling story about the things that are important to me. I do not want to write my story like a factual documentary, weighing all the pros and cons of my experience, but instead tell the uplifting story of the wonder of my own life. It's a way to transform my life from what it is now to what I want it to be. By aligning myself with my wants, I can attract things to me by the power of the laws of the universe.

I say to my son, "Daddy loves you. Mommy loves you. Grandpa loves you, Grandma loves you, Mama loves you, Atta loves you, Peddamma loves you (and the list of people in our lives), and everyone loves you, Keshav."

With the helpful suggestions from Radhi and Prakash, as well as Anna and Akka, I have been able to assertively answer my son's questions. You've given me the support I need to fly!

I started reading another book, *A Guide for Changing Families,* to my son, and we both are learning in the process. Families are all different, and whatever it is, wherever I am, it is "just right for me!" My life is a perfect stage to help me to get to where I want to be.

Learning and Discoveries

As the saying goes, "Our world is a reflection of us." We discover more of ourselves in our interactions with others as if they were tests. These tests show how much knowledge we have grasped. Our day-to-day interactions are the

Butterfly

practical fields for us to demonstrate, reflect and discover who we are, our nature, our interests, our likes and dislikes.

Each encounter is a blessing and we gain something from our interactions. However, interactions with children help us grow in many ways much faster.

Children are pure, innocent and not manipulative, unlike adults. They don't know how to massage or mask their expressions, and they display just the way they feel. There are no shades of gray with children. They do it or don't do it. They say it or don't say it. Because of the nature of children, it becomes easy for adults to understand children and better respond to them.

Children are spontaneous. They do not think about whether to say sorry, thank you or I love you. They say or do not say it. Period. While we adults think about how to say it, when to say it and look for the appropriate moment or situation.

Kids do or do not do. They do not stay in the middle or flutter. They don't carry baggage from the past or push regrets into the future. At the end of the day they sleep happily, wake up and start a new day with a breath of freshness. Because of this attitude, they do not get bored; they continuously keep exploring new things. Kids know no limits. They keep going with renewed energy and enthusiasm.

My son is four years old now. During these four years, I discovered much more of myself than I knew before. Some discoveries are trivial, yet very thought provoking, and I wonder why I never reflected on those thoughts before. There is a right time for everything. Isn't there? I am glad I am discovering and learning so much more with my son now.

I also learned more about my positive strengths by seeing them reflected in my son. I notice the way he organizes his things, the way he puts his socks inside the shoes and arranges them in a perfect line; the way he brushes his teeth

Raising My Son

without splashing a lot of water. I also see my good feelings and high energies permeating him very quickly.

My first book reading session with 20 four-year-old children was like soaking up all the creative energy, fully demanding to be in the moment, asking questions galore.

As I was reading and talking about different families, one child asked, "Doesn't Keshav have a daddy?" And I answered, "His daddy is not here. He just stays with his mama."

Then he said, "I have two daddies and one mama." We reiterated that we all have different types of families. I'm glad it came up and I answered well and in good cheer. All the children got to hear it in front of Keshav and his teachers. Hopefully now we will not have to go through any more discomfort at school.

The children asked for my name. Each of them started saying their moms' names. As I read that we like different things, and sometimes they could be the same things, they started saying, "I like strawberries," "I like bananas," "I like vegetables," "Why doesn't Keshav bring his lunch?" "Doesn't he have a lunch box?" Some children asked questions about the topic I read, but others were random, out-of-the-box questions on a totally different plane. Overall, it was fun and a joy to see their world.

Yes, it is indeed an amazing experience to be in the bubbling, creative world of children. They quickly grasp ideas and rapidly switch their thoughts to the current moment. It's a bit overwhelming to handle if one is not open and flexible to their pace though. It is a good push and encouragement for me to grow up to it.

I guess it is such a proud feeling to any child when their parents are involved in their school activities, as simple as just stepping in for a few minutes. Keshav's face beams. That evening on our way back he said, "Mommy, you did an excellent job reading!" When I telephoned my father later that day, my son told his Tata (grandpa), "My mommy read very, very good."

Now I am excited and want to have more of these experiences. I did many more of those book readings.

Are children creative? When Keshav was three years old, he knocked my socks off. Here's the conversation.

Son: Mama, you look like zebra.
Me: Zebra? Why do you think so?
Son: Because, because, you look like a horse.
Me: Horse?
Son: You look like a cow....

When I shared this during my speech in Toastmasters, in the Q&A session, Jocelyn asked me, "Did you ever figure out why you look like a zebra, a horse or a cow?"

I couldn't stop laughing and said, "I haven't. I would probably leave it as a pleasant mystery and remain in wonder."

That is another reason children are bubbly and cherubic; they don't get bogged down with reasons. They just keep going.

Our Thoughts Change

Do you remember hearing the phrases, "Her mind is like a chameleon's mind," or "I have no idea what he's going to do next"?

Aren't all our thoughts changing? It is the nature of the mind to think of various thoughts. The mind has the freedom to wander. As a matter of fact, there isn't anything in the universe that does not change—certainly not a live person. If something is not changing, it's probably dead.

This is a fact. You change, I change, and the world changes. But the irony is, we expect certain things outside of us not to change and to be the way we expect them to be. When Keshav was two years old, he used to say, "Amma, juice. Amma, juice..."

I asked, "Are you sure?"

"Yes!" was his answer, with a big enthusiastic nod.

So I walked to the pantry, grabbed a juice box, took out the straw and pierced the juice box. He watched what I was doing with excitement to receive the juice box.

But when I give it to him, he says, "No."

"What?"

Waving his hand horizontally, he repeats, "No, Amma, no …"

No. A big, blunt no. No persuading helps, nor scolding, nor screaming. Finally I give up and let it go.

For the first few times this happened, I convinced myself that he didn't know what he was asking for; and he realized it only after I gave it to him.

But the next time he asked for milk, something he clearly knows and likes, it was the same story. He said "No" after I gave it to him, and even refused to hold it.

One fine Saturday morning, I realized something interesting. I was getting my breakfast ready. I toasted two slices of whole-grain bread, took out of the refrigerator my favorite spread. And just as I was opening the lid, I thought, *Hey, why not enjoy a peanut butter and honey sandwich today.* I put back my butter spread in the refrigerator, made the sandwich and relished every bite of it, and savored a warm cup of coffee.

Suddenly a thought flashed through my mind. "I changed my mind to eat a peanut butter sandwich instead of butter topped toasted bread within a second's flash." There is no big reason why I had to eat one over the other one. I like both of them equally. It's a simple illustration of how a human mind can change in the flash of an eyelid. There were no obvious reasons for my choice. Sometimes we just do what we feel in the moment. I felt like eating a peanut butter and honey sandwich, I ate it and enjoyed it. It could be the same with my son refusing to drink juice or milk after I brought it to him.

Another example involves choosing a restaurant with my son. I decide where to go and tell my son. Sometimes he is fine with my choice, and sometimes he is not; he wants to go to some other place. Once in a while, I am okay with the change in plans but not always. The times when I have already preset my mind and have a craving for a particular food, I am really not okay, and I insist on going to the place of my choice. Yet, sometimes I give up, thinking it is much easier and pleasant to go to my son's choice of restaurant instead of making a big fuss to go to the place I want. I won't be happy to go to this other place, yet I go.

Then we started to set up rules. Now I am going by your choice, but next time we will go to my choice.

Let's stop for a second and look back. Were there any obvious reasons why I didn't eat bread with butter the other day, or why my son changed his mind in what he wanted to eat? Most likely there are no obvious reasons, and the same is true here. In the third example I can't infer that because my son wants to go to a different place to eat that he does not love me or does not care for me. Rather it is an independent decision and he wants to execute his choice. Similarly, when I want to go with my choice it doesn't mean that I don't love my son. I simply felt like going to that particular restaurant in that moment.

Reflecting on this example it brought to my awareness that sometimes our tastes differ, and each person has their own preferences and choices in any moment. This is how we learn to compromise, and also experience a sense of gratification in giving. There are times when Keshav offers me with pleasure what I like. That is the joy in mutual give and take.

And there are times when we both bounce back and enjoy the other person's choice. It is similar to how the restaurant didn't have the dish we ordered at that particular time, and because of it we had an opportunity to savor another new yummy dish.

When we learn to accept things as they are, that our minds are seeking different things at different times and not link things together, or make judgments, we live a happier life.

It's much easier to accept our own changing mind rather than that of others. However, by understanding the core basics of a human mind, and its tendency to change, we can learn to accept other people's changing expressions too.

Thanks to my little one who helped me ponder on this and discover this truth. Our mind does change, and change is constant. Let's learn to accept it, and the changing world as it is, without making judgments. It helps us to live with joy and bliss.

A Healing Balm for a Child—a Hug

It was in December of 2011 that I was home for three days with Keshav because he had an ear infection. I had to keep a careful watch over him to take care of his needs more attentively, giving him timely medicine, lots of fluids and appropriate food.

It was the first day of these three days. He was cranky and had a few short tantrums. He asked for pongal (made with rice and moong dal) for lunch, one of his favorites. I noticed that when I ask him what he wants to eat, cook it at just the right time and serve him right off the stove, he loves eating and finishes it quickly.

This day, Keshav checked to see if his lunch was ready. The pressure cooker has just cooled down enough to open the lid. And I was about to put in a bowl when he suddenly started to cry. "What happened, Keshav? Is something hurting? Are you okay? Do you want something?"

But I got no answer; he just continued to cry non-stop.

I didn't know how to console him so I sat quietly for a few minutes, trying to be peaceful myself and think of what to do. Then I went to him, took him in my arms gently and with a hug said, "I love you, Keshav. Everyone loves you" in a soft voice. I couldn't believe how miraculously it worked.

He just stopped his loud crying and said, "I love my mama."

Then I knew that his cry was more for love and comfort than anything else. He asked for his food and ate it happily.

I am sure most moms are aware of this magic combination—a hug and the words, "I love you."

I believe it is important to assure our children by saying very often that we love them and accept them no matter what. It means a lot to them. In turn, we help them grow into stronger kids with greater self-esteem and greater values.

An infant probably lives in unconditional trust and security in the parental bonding. As the child starts growing and learns to discern good/bad, correct/incorrect, acceptable/unacceptable behaviors, actions, attitudes and qualities, the feeling of love starts getting somewhat confusing. My parents love me when I do good things, things they like, the way they like things to be done, but not otherwise might be their thought.

It is so important to tell our children that we always love them no matter what. It reminds me of a popular saying: "Always find fault with the act or behavior, never with the person."

When we correct our children about an inappropriate action, let's limit the fault to the specific action. End the conversation by saying, "I love you." Some think that this way of mending an inappropriate action, followed by expressing

"I love you" with a hug could be confusing to the child or not drive the point home.

But this is not the case. It is, in fact, a very effective way and conveys the point really well, and helps the child to correct themselves in a positive, loving, nurturing, secured environment—in the environment of belongingness and in the positive energy of love. As parents we should help our children to learn from their mistakes, and understand their boundaries. We also need to make it clear that we still love and care for them and are only disapproving their inappropriate actions.

We all grow, learn and mend better in a supportive, positive, loving environment, don't we? Then why wouldn't such environments help our children? It indeed helps in many greater ways.

I am amazed to watch the better receptivity in even my 3-year-old son when I remember to do it this way. He seems more receptive and encouraged to follow through in correcting his ways. The payoff for me, in addition to teaching him right ways, is to be in greater positive energy with well-balanced poise. When I just corrected the behavior without ending with "I love you," the result is not the same. I guess another important word is "love" itself. When we say "I love you" to someone, we send that positive energy of love, and it dissolves all the negative energies and revs up the constructive positive energy within both the giver and the receiver.

What applies to children also applies to us adults as well. We all still have that child-spirit in us, craving what children crave. We want to be lifted up with the same good feelings. We crave love as well. Let the love, our true nature, flow freely. It gives so much inner strength to be love, to love and to be loved.

To reiterate what I said before, I think it is really important to assure our kids by saying very often that we love them and accept them lovingly no matter what. It means a lot to them. In turn, we are helping them grow into stronger adults with greater self-esteem and greater values.

COOKING—AN EXPRESSION OF LOVE

One day Vanita, my dear friend, said, "Cooking indeed is a communication expression."

How many times do we remember other people for what they cooked for us? Or people remember us for what we cooked and served them? Don't these leave us with such good feelings and expressions of love and warmth? How would we feel when our loved one says, "You made the food even tastier today, as you added your love"?

I love the feeling I get when Keshav loves what I cook for him. He loves pappu (yellow lentils), an all-time favorite with Indian children. It is such a simple dish to make, and the very first solid food introduced to most babies—pappu with annam (cooked rice) and neyyi (clarified butter). The next two favorites of Keshav's are sambhar and zucchini curry. Now these two became my signature items, and whoever ate the ones I made loved them, with no exceptions. I will share the recipes for them here:

Pappu or Mudda Pappu (yellow lentils)

Ingredients: Kandi pappu or yellow dal - 1 cup; salt to taste

Directions:
Wash and rinse kandi pappu
Add two cups of water and pressure cook for two whistles; lower the flame to one level below medium, and turn off the stove in five minutes. Once the pressure cooker loses its steam (in about 10 minutes), take out the cooked dal, mash it with a spoon, and add salt to taste. Serve it with cooked white rice and ghee (clarified butter).

Raising My Son

Zucchini Curry

I didn't know zucchini while in India. Most Indians still may not cook it. So, I make it as a special item for all my guests. The trick is to not overcook it or mash it. It has to be handled gently.

Ingredients:
3 medium sized zucchinis: diced to cubes
1/2 medium sized red onion, cut into semi-circles
1 tsp. mustard seeds
1 tsp. cumin seeds
1 clove of garlic: pressed
1 dry red chili
1 string of curry leaves
1 tbsp. of peanut powder (directions for this too at the bottom)
pinch of turmeric
1/2 tsp. red chili powder
salt to taste
2 tbsp. of canola oil

Directions:
Keep a stir-fry pan on medium heat
Add oil
After oil warms up, add mustard seeds, and let them splutter
Add cumin and let them splutter
Add garlic clove, stir a bit
Break the red chili into two and add
Add onions, and mix well
Add curry leaves, turmeric and mix well
Add zucchini pieces, mix well
Add salt to taste, chili powder and mix well
Increase the heat to medium high, cover with lid, and simmer for five minutes
Take off the lid, stir gently to turn the pieces, and cook for five more minutes uncovered

BUTTERFLY

Sprinkle peanut powder, and mix well
Lower the heat to medium low, cover and simmer for one to two minutes

Enjoy with chapatis (wheat tortillas) or brown/white rice

Peanut Powder

Ingredients:
1/2 cup raw peanuts
1 tbsp. coriander seeds
1 tsp. cumin
2 dried red chilies
2 tbsp. dry coconut powder
salt to taste

Directions:
Fry all these golden brown until you smell a nice roasted aroma
Cool
Blend them coarse in a coffee blender
You could save it in an airtight container, refrigerate and use it later
    (This makes much more than what is needed for the recipe)

Sambhar is a very popular dish in South Indian cuisine

Ingredients:
Vegetables:
1 medium sized red onion: 1/2" width semi-circles
1 medium sized green bell pepper: 1"x1" cubes
1 medium sized tomato: cut to 1"x1" cubes
2 medium sized carrots: peeled and cut to quarters and 2" long
10 small radishes: halved
10 okra: cut into 2" length pieces

Raising My Son

2 tbsp. canola oil
¼ tsp. turmeric
½ tsp. chili powder
1 tbsp. sambhar powder
pinch of asafoetida
1.5 cups kandi pappu (yellow dal)
tamarind, about one key lime sized ball: wash, soak, squeeze juice from pulp and set aside

For talimpu (seasoning)
2 crushed garlic cloves
1 tsp. of grated fresh ginger (I like the flavor; but it is optional)
A string of curry leaves
½ tsp. mustard seeds
½ tsp. cumin
¼ tsp. fenugreek
½ tsp. urad dal
pinch of asafoetida

Directions:
Pressure cook kandi pappu with three cups of water until two whistles
I use a deep pan, 5-quart sauce pan
Put on stove, once the pan warms up, add oil
After the oil is warmed up, add the cut vegetables
Add turmeric and salt to taste and mix and let the vegetables cook for two minutes
Add chili powder, sambhar powder and mix and cook for a minute
(Let the vegetables absorb the little salt and spice)

Then add two to three liters of water; add the tamarind juice, cover and let the water boil and cook the vegetables to firm but tender

Then add cooked dal, salt to taste and chili powder to taste (if not enough)
Let the whole thing boil until you see pongu (bubbling) and it loses the raw smell

Do the seasoning in a small pan
Heat oil until sizzling
Add seasoning ingredients one after the other—mustard seeds, fenugreek, cumin, urad dal, garlic, curry leaves, asafoetida, ginger
Fry for 30 to 40 seconds, roasted to golden brown but not burnt

Add to the dal, simmer for a minute, and enjoy with rice

Heartfelt Memories

I enjoy humor and am always looking to be as humorous as I can be. When I listen to other speakers in Toastmasters, I realized that including something fun is really important to put the audience at ease and to help them absorb the message better. I had no idea what funny lines I could add to my speeches and checking online resources for humor was a waste of time. I can only get to clean, simple humor, so I began making notes of some of the funny experiences I run into with my son and save them in my fun-humor collection file. They bring a smile to my face every time I share them with someone. I hope you enjoy them as much as I do.

2/14/12—Valentine's Day

Keshav was excited to celebrate Valentine's Day at school. The night before the party, we wrote his name and put stickers on the little Valentine cards and had fun doing it.

I asked him, "Valentine antee enti Keshav?" (What does Valentine mean, Keshav?) He put his hand on his chest and said, "Valentine is heart; happy Valentine heart."

It was so funny watching him say it. I asked him several times and I laughed at his answer, and he laughed with me each time.

Later when he called up to wish his mama (my Anna), atta (my Vadina), and Siddu (his cousin) a happy Valentine's Day, he said, "Happy Valentine's heart!"

~~~~~~~~~~

2011—My Birthday

"Today is my birthday, Keshav. What shall we do?" Immediately, this 3-year-old said, "We will go to a blue place, Amma."

Later, I figured out that by blue place he meant "his favorite place" because blue is his favorite color.

When Akka asked what we were doing, I wrote to her in addition to the above:

For Keshav, birthdays mean "a place to celebrate." He said we will go to a "blue birthday place." I have to look out for a blue place now. He enjoys eating out, so we will both go out for dinner tonight, my treat for Keshav on my birthday! And of course it makes such a big difference in my life to have him with me.

12/2/11—Morning Prayer

I look at Keshav every morning on our way to his school, to make sure he is attentive to what I am saying. "God is with us to help us with everything we want. Let's make today_____."

Then I pause for him to say, "A miraculous day" (of course he still can't say the word "miraculous" very clearly yet, but says it in his own sweet voice).

Then he continues by himself, or with my cues.

Will do three miracles" (or sometimes five or 20—a random number he picks) or he picks a color of his choice, maybe the color of the shirt he is wearing. "Will do 'blue' miracles."

It's a fun exercise I do every day with him. It puts us into high, bubbly spirits.

It's just amazing to watch how creative and open-minded kids are. As an adult my answers seem monotonous, while he comes up with creative ideas of numbers and colors of miracles. It's a pleasant feeling to see him being creative.

~~~~~~~~

2/20/12-Candlelit Dinner

On this day, I felt like doing something special for myself and had a candlelit dinner. Keshav joined me, and when we finally finished, he blew out the candle. Whenever I light a candle or he sees one, he says "birthday candle cake." For him, those three are associated. Lighting a candle is like placing candles on a birthday cake; just as he associates a "blue place" with his favorite color.

~~~~~~~~

5/29/12—Nature

Saturday we went to a park named Wildwood Park. It had a lake and a walking trail in the woods. It was pleasant to spend just enough time for both of us to have a change. Keshav was excited to see the ducks and butterflies flying around, and he enjoyed the walk. Before we left, he ran back quickly, saying, "Mama, let me see the chocolate water one more time!" I didn't really get it at first, but the water did look somewhat brown—like chocolate.

~~~~~~~~

4/10/13—Tulips

On our way to Keshav's school, pointing at the red tulips, I said, "Keshav, look at those beautiful red tulips."

With a puzzled face, he said, "What tulips?"

Thinking he didn't see the flowers, I pointed my fingers and showed, "Those are tulips."

"Tulips, is it their first name?"

Ah, not finding a quick answer, hesitatingly I said, "Yeah."

"What is their last name?"

Now I had to be spontaneous. I said, "Plant."

~~~~~~~~

3/16/13—Age

At 4 years old, Keshav is learning numbers in pre-kindergarten. He asked me, "Mommy, how old are you?"

I answered, "38."

"What comes next?"

I said, "39."

"And then?"

"40."

From 41 he picked up the pattern and started counting, 41, 42, 43 …. 48, 49 and 40-10.

~~~~~~~~

9/7/12—Reading

The most impressive part of the weekend was watching Keshav reading the book *Goldilocks and the Three Bears*. He is becoming a very interesting story reader and a story-teller! His teacher mentioned to me that he loved that book, and so I borrowed two different versions of it from the library. And he thoroughly enjoyed reading both of them. I was giggling inside with his narration. Almost all the pages began with, "Once upon a time…." The other exciting sentence for both him and me was: "It was not too hot, or too cold. It was just right!" Somehow it particularly stood out and was his best phrase in reading that story. I love this phrase and call it the Goldilocks phrase. Every time I say it, a pleasant smile comes to my face.

10/26/12—A Favorite Word

I read "Cock-a-doodle-do" to my son's class, and the next day I got a note from his teacher: When we got up from our nap today, they were all saying "cockle-doodle-do." The students must have been engaged and enjoyed the book.

Keshav and I both love reading this book and especially saying, "cock-a-doodle-do." During weekends if I sleep late, he comes to my bed in order to wake me up by saying "cock-a-doodle-do."

10/03/12—Negotiation

I once gave a speech on negotiation. Here was my opening story. "I want some Oreo cookies, Mommy," says my sleepy 4-year-old one morning, still rubbing his eyes. Maybe he is still in his dreams....

"First brush your teeth and eat your cereal."

"Can I have my Oreos then?"

I give in, "Okay." Kids know how to negotiate.

11/02/12—Logical Answer

During a parent teacher conference, his teacher was telling me about Keshav's test.

I said, "Birds fly, fish_____".

He answered, "Fish drink water."
I was expecting "fish swim," she said with a smile.

1/7/12—Sentences
Last night I was in the kitchen doing something. I was alarmed by a soft touch on my back. I didn't notice Keshav coming into the room.
With a jerk, I said, "You scared me, Keshav."
"I am not a dinosaur, Mommy", he said with the most innocent expression and all sorts of wild gestures.
I burst into laughter. It was one of his first complete sentences.

3/01/13: Orange
Someone said that I didn't pronounce the word "orange" well and that they didn't hear the "r" sound, so I asked Keshav to tell me how to say "orange." He did it well every time I asked.
Then I said, "You are so little and do it correctly all the time. Mom is so big, yet she doesn't know how to do it well and wonders if she is doing it right or not. Why do you think she doesn't know?"
His answer was, "I think you need to get back to 4 like me to say it correctly." I couldn't stop laughing.

2/10/13—The Core
I love what my 4-year-old says to me when I am upset with him.

BUTTERFLY

"Mommy, let's pray to God to make our minds g.o.o.d."

Surely doing this bounces us both into our peaceful spirits. He reminded me that I believe in making a connection to the core-peace within us.

8/20/12—Mixing the Lyrics

Recently, Keshav was singing a song over and over in joyful spirits, "Life is like a four! Life is like a four!" I told him that I liked hearing his song and asked for the words.

Then I asked, "Who taught you this song, Keshav?"

With a blush, he said, "My mama."

I was kind of surprised, as I didn't recognize the song. Then it struck me. While I get ready in the morning, I sing, "Life is so very good. Life loves me, enthusiasm loves me," and this boy converted it to "Life is like a four!"

Another day he was repeating the word "thank you": "Thank you for my toys. Thank you for birthday...." I realized that he does this when he is by himself. He has his own list of gratitude's. He uses the word "beautiful" many times and with all big smiles. If he can't get to sleep sometimes, he says to me, "Mama, I want to tell you something beautiful." He calls me "Sweetie Mama" when he really wants me to say "yes" to what he wants. Kids are so smart and beautifully sweet.

~~~~~~~~~

I'm glad I am infusing positive energy in him!

Final Thoughts

I would like to share a few important principles that helped me tremendously in my journey:

1. **Accepting 100 percent responsibility** ~ Remember the saying, "No risk, no gain"? Accepting responsibility helps us to stretch in many ways. With responsibility comes commitment. When we accept the responsibility, we will automatically do whatever is necessary to hold the responsibility. It could involve facing challenges, struggles, the push and plunge. All this will help us to shape into a powerful person with greater courage and strength. The responsibility we accept comes in various relationship roles we hold within the circle of family, career and community. The greater the responsibility we accept, the more lives we touch and serve and the more enriched we become. Our relationships give us enormous strength, support and a sense of belonging to each other. Accepting 100 percent responsibility is the key to making our lives happen *for* us.

2. **Ask and receive** ~ There are people willing to help us grow and succeed if we step out and ask for what we want and need. Asking may not be easy for some. Some are afraid to simply step out and ask for fear of rejection. This was true for me until I felt that circumstances compelled me to step outside my comfort zone. I received help in many ways from countless people, to whom I am so thankful. My life would have been very different if I

BUTTERFLY

hadn't stepped out and asked for help. I would not have held the same gratitude for them and would not have shared the rich mutual feelings we now hold. Without the help I received I wouldn't have been the person I am today. I grew into a better person, in an accelerated way, just because of the help I received. And most of the time, whoever helped me did so happily.

Now I know that there is nothing to lose by asking, even if we do not receive what we ask for in that moment. If we truly need something, we will almost certainly receive it sometime, in some form, in totally unexpected ways. We just have to be open to receive it. Once I was criticized and accused of using people by asking for help. Nevertheless, I still admire myself for stepping out and asking for possible help. It depends purely on the intent behind seeking the help. As long as our intentions are not selfish and we have no evil intent, there is nothing wrong in asking for help.

3. **Work on Passions** ~ I can't express in mere words how good I felt when I started blogging and started sharing my passionate work—writing. I received great encouragement and support from my blog readers. Each of them touched me in a special way. Their encouragement was the fuel—stirring in me a burning desire to write. It even boosted my self-esteem and confidence and acted as a steppingstone to propel me out of my comfort zone and connect to others with relative ease. My world soon started getting bigger, brighter and prettier! I was able to connect with my family and friends on a much more positive, stimulating and productive way.

The time we spend on our passions surely fills us with bliss, keeping us in the present moment. By sharing our passions we spread that joy to others. Recently, during the Youth Leadership Program, Jocelyn, my fellow

Final Thoughts

Toastmaster and I were conducting, Katie said, "I sing because it makes me happy to sing. I sing to others to share my happiness. I may never sing for my profession, or for a college degree, yet I will do it for my lifetime as I enjoy doing it." What a joy and inspiration it is to hear this from a 16-year-old girl!

If you haven't already done so, please start working on your passions today. When we start working on our passions, we naturally feel uplifted, alive and agile. Let's work on our passions, for the *joy* of doing, not for the *fruits* of the doing. The fruits will flow to us naturally and could surprise us amazingly.

If I—a shy girl—who used to go unnoticed during my school and college days, am able to inspire others, I definitely know you can do it too. Each of us is unique. Please take some time to sincerely discover your passions, and start working on them. The world definitely needs you and is desperately waiting to be touched by you. Reach out and touch others with your unique abilities, talents and passions.

4. **Team Up and Co-create** ~ In reality, there is not even one thing that we enjoy in this moment which is totally created by us. The book you are reading, for example, is a co-creation of many minds and hearts. The meal you had for your lunch today involved the collaborative work of hundreds or even thousands of people behind the scenes; the chair you are sitting on, the car you drive, the house in which you are living, you name it. It takes a team.

Let us make use of other people's skills to *leverage* us. Share our skills and expertise so that others can leverage them. Gracefully enjoy the flow of both giving and receiving; when we help others to grow, we grow as well.

We grow by being coached but we can grow equally, or even more, by coaching someone else. Like trees and

BUTTERFLY

shrubs, both the coached and coach grow in different ways. If we limit our joy to ourselves, it is like enjoying the apples we grew. By sharing our fruits with others and being receptive to others' fruits, together we can enjoy the fruits of apples, oranges and every single fruit ever grown. The familiar acronym for TEAM is "together everyone achieves more."

Let us Co-create and reap the benefits of the inter-connectedness. Ask and receive. Step up to volunteer and to offer help. Savor the multi-flavors and multi-colors of our co-creation.

5. **Encouragers, Supporters, Inspirers** ~ Can you count on someone who created "an eager want" in you to plunge into something new? This person may have believed in you more than you believed in yourself. They saw beyond who you are to the person you could become. They may have inspired you to go for something big.

   I am very blessed to have good support and encouragement from my family, friends and Toastmasters.

   Ravindra is one of my special friends who created a burning desire in me to transform my writings and put them to good use. Without his encouragement and belief in me, I would never have brought my writing skills into the light.

   It is very important to have encouragers, supporters and inspirers who give us a push to raise our limits and stretch ourselves.

   Do you have encouragers, supporters and inspirers in your life? Be thankful and always stay connected to them. We cross paths with many people. Some touch us and lift us up beyond our imaginations, but they may not stay by our sides forever, which is okay. With our growing needs, we have to constantly and consistently renew and replenish our encouragers, supporters and inspirers.

Final Thoughts

Let us find our encouragers, and become an encourager to someone ourselves. Let us create an eager want in others to become their best possible self.

6. **Do and Surrender** ~ Do whatever you want and then surrender. Think whatever you want and then surrender. Feel whatever you want and then surrender. That helps us in keeping our mind free and clear. Thus enabling us to fully enjoy the present moment. By practicing letting go, we can embrace the dualities of the world, accept everything as it is and glide through life gracefully in love, joy, peace and bliss.

7. **Each Encounter is a Blessing** ~ Every person we encounter in our life is a blessing. Some people are easy to love and connect with. Some are not so easy. And some even push our buttons. Yet, each person we have encountered is a gift and a blessing, as each has helped us to discover certain parts of ourselves more clearly. Each encounter has brought to our awareness what we like, what we resonate with, what makes us excited, what we would like to change, what we cannot tolerate. It doesn't matter if the experience is pleasant or unpleasant; each has been a learning experience, and we grew because of it. I am thankful to each person and each situation I've experienced, only because of them I grew into the person I am today.

May we all live by these words: "Love is like a butterfly: It goes where it pleases and it pleases wherever it goes."

Glossary of Telugu terms

Note: The Bhagavad Gita, or Gita for short, is a Hindu holy scripture. The meaning of Bhagavad Gita is "Song of the Lord." Gita is the sublime message delivered by the omnipotent Supreme-Soul, Lord Krishna, to the warrior Arjuna on the eve of a battle between the two aspirant teams, the Pandavas and the Kauravas. The Pandavas and the Kauravas metaphorically represent the good and evil teams respectively. Arjuna is the lead warrior of the Pandava team. The Gita was originally written in Sanskrit. Later, it was translated into English and many other Indian languages. The Gita verses I quoted in Part 3—Spiritual Transformation are in Sanskrit. I did not give the meaning of the Sanskrit words but rather the English translation underneath the verses.

Here is a glossary of Telugu words used in this book:

Akka	elder sister
Amma	mother
Ammamma	mom's mom
ammayi	girl
Anna	elder brother
Bavagaru	brother-in-law
bellam	jaggery, concentrated sugar made from sugar cane juice
jada	plait
jilakara	cumin

BUTTERFLY

kalyanam	marriage
kodalu	daughter-in-law
kumkuma	vermilion powder
Mama	mom's bother
Mamalu	mom's brothers; plural of mama
mamidakulu	mango leaves
manavaraalu	granddaughter
moodu	three
mudulu	knots
muhurtham	an auspicious set time
neyyi	clarified butter
pappu	cooked yellow dal
pasupu	turmeric
pattu cheera	silk sari
pedda	elder
pelli	marriage
pelli chupulu	the bride seeing ceremony
pelli mandapam	wedding stage
Pellilla perayya	a marriage mediator
Pinni	mom's sisters
Pinnilu	mom's sisters (plural of pinni)
puvvulu	flowers
rasam	South Indian soup traditionally prepared using tamarind juice as a base
sari	a traditional Indian woman's dress
shamiana	wedding tent
Tata	grandpa
thalambralu	rice grains mixed with turmeric, vermilion powder and flower petals

Glossary of Telugu terms

thilakam	bindi, a red dot put on the forehead between the eyebrows; it could also be put in a special shape other than a circle
Vadina	sister-in-law

Acknowledgements

I want to thank the people involved in co-creating this book. Dr. Ralph Hillman, my voice coach, suggested I contact Jan Whalen to assist me in writing and organizing the content of my book. Without Jan's help, there is no way my book would have been tuned, refined and polished into this beautiful form. She not only assisted in editing, but she also gave me that encouraging boost of positive energy needed to keep the writing flowing with such joy. She patiently answered my questions and diffused the many fluttering feelings I encountered in the process. She is a blessing sent my way in this journey.

Jan brought together a team of professionals to assist with this book. I would like to thank cover designers Gerry Castro and Crystal McMahon, and page designer Quality Data Mill, Pvt. Ltd. I thank them for using their skills to package this book so beautifully and for making it possible to get into your hands. I thoroughly enjoyed working with them, and I believe this book is a beautiful co-creation due to the passionate work of the entire team.

Thank you to my friend Ravindra, who encouraged me to make use of my writing skills, and who believed in my talent more than I did. He brought my passion for writing into the light. His constructive criticism and suggestions for writing a true story have been immensely valuable to me.

Thank you to my friend Purna for offering invaluable feedback and ideas during the development of this book. She invested many hours reading my manuscript several times.

Thank you to my friend Radhi for encouraging me to put effort into my passionate dreams, for sharing her passionate energies and for all the feedback she gave me in this journey.

To my friend Prakash, who shares many resonating thoughts, admires my writing and adds fuel and strength to my writing. I'm so thankful to him for the feedback and support he provided throughout this journey.

Thank you to Shivani who voluntarily pitched in to assist in the editing of my manuscript and for sharing her thoughts.

Thank you to my college mates, Facebook friends and my blog readers who encouraged and supported my writing in many ways. You helped me muster the courage to publish a book and provided pointers and connections related to the book-publishing process.

Thank you to many Toastmasters, the DHS Toastmasters and especially my mentor Carey Schaller for helping me improve my writing skills by editing my written speech scripts and for helping me improve my speaking skills.

My gratitude and sincere thanks go to my work colleagues, who inspire me, guide me, encourage me and help me in many ways each day.

To my local friends who extend their helping hands on many occasions, it gives me such peace to know that I have people to count on when I need assistance.

I give my deepest appreciation and gratitude to my doctor, Dr. Robert Collins, for diligently and compassionately working on my case and whose work resulted in blessing me with a miraculous recovery from a life-threatening illness.

I am blessed with a beautiful family who loves and supports me.

To Amma, Sarada and Daddy, Ramakrishna Rao Chinta, who nurtured me with tender love and care and instilled in me

ACKNOWLEDGEMENTS

deep strength, courage and will-power. Thank you, Mom and Dad, for your unconditional love and support.

To my loving Ammamma, Vasundara Devi, who showers me to this day with her unconditional love—a pure joy to be around. She taught us many invaluable lessons by just the way she is. The first poem I ever wrote is about Ammamma.

To Jyothi Pinni who always holds a special place in my heart for the noble deeds she extends to our whole family and for the affection and care she still extends to this day.

To Anna, Vijay Bhushan, who is my role model and who, in many ways, offers the guidance and help I need. He brings me to a place of thinking clearly and simplifies the complex. He has a wonderful gift of instilling peace and calmness with his compassion and takes me to my child-spirits of laughter and fun. His wisdom and generosity always inspire me.

Thank you to my Vadina, Vasavi, who is younger in age, but who offers me guidance on any subject. She is like my encyclopedia of quick insights. Whatever I ask, she knows the answer, without even having to think. She actively gave me guidance, support, encouragement and constructive thoughts throughout this journey. She helped me feel confident with my writing.

To Akka, Jhansi Lakshmi, who is the caring, concerned sister of my childhood and who grew into our wise family doctor, ready to give medical advice any minute. She is also the family planner—the first one to send a checklist for our travel plans or any important assignments.

To Bavagaru, Ramesh Parasa, who amazes me with his strength and strong will-power and who is another family doctor to consult for any medical advice.

Thank you to my cousins Gautam and Mamata who bring proud feelings to me when I think that I have another brother who is just two months older and a little sister. Thank you, Mamata, for happily offering to help edit the book and for sharing your thoughts.

Thank you to Aunty Indira who keeps appreciating and encouraging me to write with passion in spite of the time-crunch I have.

Thank you to my other aunts and uncles who cared for me and loved me. When visiting their homes during my childhood or during vacations, they treated me like a princess. They still hold the same love for me even though I am a grown woman with my own baby.

To my niece Mona, the first baby in our family, who was a joy to hold and cherish. She instilled confidence that I can talk to and bathe a baby. As she grew, I was amazed how she sang songs she heard with ease, and later she gave me tips to improve my own singing.

To my niece Sindhu, who permeated joy with her arrival, thus lowering our anxiety during the unknown times of my life-threatening illness. She offers the same comfort to this day and is incredibly thoughtful—a sage for her age.

To my nephews Abhi and Pranav who always bring a contrast from our nieces and who don't shower their love with hugs and cuddles, but carry so much within their hearts.

To my son Keshav who is pure joy and mystery and who is the wonder of my life. At times he pushes my buttons and makes me look into myself more deeply to transform me, and he is my biggest teacher! Thank you, Keshav, for understanding my long nights at the computer and forgoing many times we could have spent together.

In naming some I might have missed many others. I give my heartfelt gratitude and thank you to all my well-wishers and to all those who touched my life and made me into a better person.

ACKNOWLEDGEMENTS

This book represents the collaborative co-creation of many hearts and minds. Without the encouragement, support, enthusiasm and best wishes it would not have been possible.

Thank you all so very much for the gifts that you have given me. I love you all so dearly.

Ultimately, my heart is filled with gratitude to the Divine Creator for the intuitive and divine guidance I was given throughout this journey and for sending me all the help, guidance and people I needed to complete this book.

About the Author

Aruna Chinta lives in Little Rock, Arkansas, with her four year old son. She works for the Arkansas Teacher Retirement System (ATRS) as a senior programmer. Being a part of the ATRS team, with so many wonderful hearts and minds, is one of her blessings. Born and raised in India, she has a bachelor's degree in engineering. She came to the United States at the age of 22 to pursue her master's degree in computer science. However, after one year, she wanted to take up a full-time job rather than focusing on her master's. So she started her career as a software programmer and have continued in the same field ever since.

An avid reader, passionate writer and an active Toastmaster, Aruna is enthusiastic about self-improvement, especially in regards to public speaking. She's the 2012–13 president of DHS Toastmasters and feels it's "a rewarding experience to see others grow and lead."

She's a blogger and welcomes you to follow her blog at Blog.ToughTimesNeverLast.com.

Namaste!